The Bariatric Foodie Breakfast Book

Ordering Information:
Quantity sales. Special discounts are available on quantity purchases by corporations, associations and others. Book signings and appearances can be arranged directly by the author by contacting (443) 486-2301 or bariatricfoodie@yahoo.com.

www.BariatricFoodie.com

Printed in the United States of America.

The Bariatric Foodie Breakfast Book.

ISBN: 978-0-9910770-2-1

Table of Contents

Acknowledgments

There are so many people to thank for the making of this book that I was hesitant to do a dedication page for fear of forgetting someone. My compromise is this: first, I'm going to thank anyone I may have forgotten below!

First and foremost, I want to thank my late mother, Rikki Cox. She instilled in me a love of food and cooking that endures today. She also helped me come to the realization that having weight-loss surgery does not mean I have to stop loving food! She also pushed me to use my writing in my process to better health. I love you always and forever, plus two more days!

Special thanks also go out to my unofficial "publications department." To Kelly and Denise, whose editing skills have exponentially increased your chances of recipe success. To Margaret, who not only loaned her kitchen and culinary expertise to recipe testing, but also taught me how to make cheese! To Pam who gave Bariatric Foodie's books their unique and appealing visual identity. There's a reason you are my VP of Common Sense and my very good friend! To Julia, who not only typeset this book, but listened to me whine, and lament, and theorize. She tested recipes and taste-tested recipes, all while serving in other, very demanding (one might call them "minion-like") roles at Bariatric Foodie.

Then there's also a few special Foodies I'd like to shout out. To Sue, Linda and Cheryl, thank you for responding to the call and sharing your wonderful recipes with the Foodie Nation! I'd also like to give a shout-out to a very special Foodie, Ruth, who I chose to get the very first copy of this book, because she takes time out of each and every day to help people on the Bariatric Foodie Facebook Page by answering questions and being an encouraging voice.

Last, but not least, to the entire #FoodieNation. You all inspire me to keep doing what I do and I thank you from the bottom of my heart. Bariatric Foodie is part of what makes life satisfying for me and your encouragement, feedback, challenges, pictures, problems, successes and questions are a treasured part of my every day. If I've ever sounded like a friend to you in my writing, it is because you were first a very dear friend to me.

I hope you enjoy this book! And if not…you know where to find me to tell me about it.

Now go on…play with your food!

You Don't Eat Breakfast, Do You?

Nope. I can see it in your eyes. Or rather the way you looked away ever so quickly when I asked the question. You, my friend, are a serial breakfast skipper, aren't you?

Wait...come closer. Maybe not. Maybe you've been doing a protein drink or something small but want breakfast to feel more like breakfast. Or maybe that grimace you just gave me means you're plain confused by the concept of a healthy breakfast altogether!

Not to worry, I'm here to help!

But first, let me take a step back and introduce myself. My name is Nikki, but most people simply call me Nik (True fact: Nikki is the actual name on my birth certificate! Not that you'd want to stalk me or anything.). Since 2009, I've run a food blog called *Bariatric Foodie* (bariatricfoodie.com) that helps people learn to "play with their food."

"Play with their food?" Yes, play with their food.

You see, in 2008 I had Roux-en-Y gastric bypass surgery and, as a result, couldn't eat very much. In that first year, I also had the added burden of nearly everything making me sick! I like to call that my "dark year." It was very depressing to think that I'd never enjoy food again, which is honestly what I believed. Until I started playing with my food!

I realized that the trick to eating healthfully was not giving up every food I love, but learning to make the dishes I love with better ingredients, better cooking methods and to keep an open mind to the form of them - y'know, playing with my food!

But breakfast is tricky for the average weight loss surgery post-op. If you're reading this, you probably had bariatric surgery (the bariatric in the book name and all...). Raise your hand if you feel a little queasy in the morning.

(I bet you actually physically raised your hand didn't you? No worries, I won't judge, but put your hand down fast! Someone might be watching!)

That's not unusual. Many post-ops feel that way for quite some time after surgery. For my part, I actually "trained" my stomach to accept food in the morning (because that's when I am most likely to work out and, frankly, I have no desire to die on a treadmill) but short of doing that, breakfast can be kind of rough.

You know one thing that has always fascinated me about breakfast, though? People seem to have very clear ideas about what is and is not breakfast food. Eggs, yes. Bacon, yes. Pancakes, yes. Pot roast? No!

But the truth of the matter is that it doesn't really matter whether your breakfast consists of eggs and bacon or pot roast. That's why I hope the ideas in this book will inspire you to re-think your own breakfasts. There's traditional recipes (omelets, frittatas and, yes, even pancakes!) but there are also some fun takes on breakfast foods that even make them dinner-worthy!

Why? Because we each like different things. And in reality all these recipes may appeal to you or none of them may appeal to you. (When's the last time a cookbook told you that? Remember, Nik always keeps it real!) I would argue that it doesn't really matter whether you like most of the recipes in this book. What matters is that they show you what you can do to make your breakfast experience better.

That's why I've loaded this book with plenty of information on food prep and variations you can use to mix up your routine. Because breakfast is hard enough without trying to eat something you hate.

Now, if you're ready to get started, buy the dang book and turn the page!

So about these recipes…

Although we have a few things to talk about before we get to the recipes, there are a few things you should know about my recipes to help you make the best use of them.

You ever followed a recipe to a "t" but you're not quite sure if the texture or flavor of your version is how it's supposed to be? That's happened to me plenty of times! To help you figure out if you're on the right track, many recipes have what I call a "Spot Check." Those are tips to help make sure you are preparing the dish according to the recipe, but sometimes they are also helpful hints on swapping one ingredient for another or a tidbit about why something is prepared the way it is. I hope you find these helpful!

There is (almost) no nutrition information for recipes in this book. That's by design. Why? Well, let's be honest. You're going to change the recipe, even if only to use a different brand of ingredient than I used (for the most part I don't indicate brands unless a specific brand is absolutely essential to the recipe). I've found that even small changes to a recipe can throw off the nutrition information (which I call "stats").

So if I'm not giving you the stats for most recipes, how can you be sure it's a good thing to eat? In my estimation you have two choices:

1. *Take my word for it!* I know you don't know me but I've staked my reputation on high protein, low/beneficial-carb cooking. Each recipe is developed with that in mind. If there are ingredients that are higher in calories or carbs, they are to help the dish be as palatable as possible.
2. *Figure out your own stats!* That can be achieved by adding up the nutrition information from all the ingredients you use and dividing by the number of servings the recipe yielded for you. I've even provided a handy space on each page to do so and a more comprehensive guide on pg. 137.

There are a few exceptions to my fairly rigid "no stats" rule. In the "Smart Carbs" section (starting on pg. 41) I give you the brand names of the ingredients I use along with the stats for the base recipe only. For everything else, you are on your own, kids! (Kidding.)

If you ever need help figuring out the nutrition information for a recipe (mine, yours, anyone's) give me a holler at bariatricfoodie@yahoo.com. Note that if you do this I will help you calculate the nutrition information. I am never, ever, ever going to do it for you.

Lastly photos. Sigh. One day I will give you a big, beautiful book with photos. For now, that costs a LOT of money to print and if it costs me money, it costs you money in the purchase price. Instead, I've created a gallery on the Bariatric Foodie Pinterest account (pinterest.com/bariatricfoodie) called "The Bariatric Foodie Breakfast Book" where you can photos of some of the recipes in this book!

Chapter One:
Breakfast Basics

In this chapter we'll discuss some of the unique challenges of breakfast from a post-op bariatric perspective, including basic food decisions you'll need to make, things that confuse most people about breakfast and how to get around the physical limitations of your surgery to incorporate breakfast into your day.

Please note that there are no general right or wrong decisions, only what is right for *you*. Read over this information, discuss it with your bariatric practice's registered dietician and come to a good decision for yourself. Then stick to it! There's always a temptation to compare your eating habits to those of other post-ops (especially if it seems to us that others are more successful than us) but in the end your body is your body. Nobody else's body works the way yours does and so you have to feed your body according to your unique needs.

Another note, as we move through this book, is that we each have our own very specific ideas about what is breakfast food and what is not. Part of that is cultural, part could have to do with our sub-culture as weight loss surgery patients (especially those of us who, like me, drink a protein shake nearly every day).

But what's special about these foods? Did we gravitate toward these foods because they give us something we specifically need in the morning or did we just wake up one day and say, "I dub thee, round piece of fried and glazed dough(nut)…breakfast food!"

It's sort of a chicken-and-egg kind of question. And I'm here to tell you that I found a million different answers which all lead me to believe that we don't really know why we eat what we eat for breakfast except that we do! That's not to discount habitual behavior. It's powerful.

Different cultures have different breakfast habits, which seem to be more governed by food availability than conscious nutrient choices. In the U.S., our choices are mostly governed by habits and familiarity. In short, we eat what we eat because it's what we've always eaten!

Sorry I couldn't give you a deeper answer! But there's lots more to talk about as we figure out what works for our personal breakfast choices, so let's journey onward!

Food Decisions of the Utmost Importance

If you're new to weight loss surgery, as you interact with others, you'll find there are various eating philosophies. Chances are you're going to experience people who fall into at least one of these schools of thought:

- **The "Frankenfooder":** This is the person who only cares about eating the least amount of calories (and least amount of fat and carbs, highest amount of protein) possible. As such, they are willing to buy foods engineered to those standards. I went through a Frankenfood phase.
- **The "Purist":** These are the polar opposite of Frankenfooders. They don't want to eat anything that has been tinkered with too much. They tend to eat whole foods (meaning foods that you buy as close to the way nature made them as possible) and rail vehemently against so-called "processed food."
- **The "Food-phobe":** This person is a person who is just plain afraid of food, afraid of their own appetite, inherently distrustful of their own decision making. These folks usually don't even keep much food in their homes if they can get away with it.
- **The "Zen God/dess":** If you are one of the above three (or have experienced a lot of them) you'll find this type a bit disconcerting. This is the person who does not track, does not freak about carbs and eats what they want to eat, in moderation.
- **"The sensible planner":** This person is mid-way between the Food-phobe and the Zen-God/dess. This is a person who doesn't necessarily freak out about every food decision but wants to be informed. Thus, this person usually tracks their intake and seeks overall balance, although they may indulge in a treat or two along the way.

I'm not saying you have to choose camps here, but you're going to experience these people (chances are you are one of these people) and each one of these types has a tendency to have an opinion about your food choices. No, it's not really any of their business, but they'll offer their opinion anyway.

So it's probably good to make some basic decisions about how you will approach food so you can make decisions with confidence, despite what anyone has to say about it. With breakfast there are several choices. Let's go over them.

Eggs

Eggs vs. liquid egg substitute

Oh, how many times have I become embroiled in this age-old debate? (Actually it's not really age-old since eggs have been around long before liquid egg substitute.)

The Frankenfooder may tell you that liquid egg substitute is best. It's lower in calories and fat than a regular egg. It's also easy to make very small portions with liquid egg substitute. Because, in all honesty, if you want to eat both the egg and the yolk, preparing half an egg without cooking the whole thing is...too much for me to think about. If you happened to have a Food-phobe around as well they'd probably agree, based on calories alone.

The Purist would probably extol the alleged dangers of processed food and point out that liquid egg substitute is engineered food at its best. I mean, what is it? Is it eggs? If it is then why do we call it "liquid egg substitute"? And, of course, the Zen person and the Sensible Planner would probably say they use both, depending on the situation.

So let's investigate this.

What is liquid egg substitute? That's a good place to start this discussion. According to one popular brand, liquid egg substitute is 99% egg whites with added beta carotene (a nutrient that also adds the yellow yolk-like color back to the whites) as well other nutrients to increase health value. So why do they call it "liquid egg substitute?"

Well, in most cases companies don't. They call them by their brand names (which I can't do here) but as a professional communicator I can say it's easier to wrap your head around liquid egg substitute than "nutritionally enhanced and tinted egg whites." So that's that.

Knowing what we now know, we must ask ourselves: Is liquid egg substitute better for you than eggs? My opinion? Probably not. Use whichever you feel most comfortable using, depending on what you think about food (and your registered dietician's advice is helpful too).

To yolk or not to yolk...

Eggs have great nutrition but many people are bothered by the amount of fat and calories in an egg's yolk. At various points in immediate history, science has swung both ways on the fat in egg yolks. At one point the scientific community deemed the fat unhealthy. These days the consensus seems to be that an egg's yolk contains essential nutrients and that we should eat them in moderation.

I'm not going to go into too much detail about the science (mostly because I'd get it completely wrong!) but I will say that, in my estimation, there are really only three good reasons to cut egg yolks out of your life if you wouldn't otherwise be inclined to:

1. If you've been advised to do so by your physician. In fact, their advice always trumps mine.
2. If the only thing keeping you from liking eggs (or feeling comfortable eating them) is the yolk. Even egg whites have great nutrition and, as you'll see in the recipes, can be a great vehicle for transforming former favorite foods. But if the yolk is holding you back, nix it!
3. If you want to eat more than one egg dish in a day. I am usually for variety but sometimes you end up with more than one egg dish in your day. While scientists are currently saying yolks have good nutrition in them, as with any food, you shouldn't eat too much of them. So if you find yourself in a "multi-egg meal day" predicament, I'd advise that you err on the side of eating egg whites in one of those meals to limit your calorie/fat intake.

I hope this short overview gives you a better idea about how you can use eggs in your eating plan. There are plenty of egg recipes in this book (starting on pg. 11). In the end, use your best judgment and play with your food!

Carbohydrates

Is starch the devil?

Many post-ops seem to think so! I've done numerous polls on my blog and social media sites and the food that seems to confound post-ops the most, scare them the most, cause the most vehement reaction is...starch.

Like with eggs, you'll get various reactions to starches. The Frankenfooder will probably have found a starch that is engineered to be higher in protein than in carbs. The Purist will usually advocate against such products and in favor of either eating a small bit of the real thing or abstaining completely. The Food-phobe probably won't touch a starch with a ten-foot pole while the Sensible Planner and the Zen God/dess are the most likely to have come to terms with healthy starches as a part of a balanced overall eating plan.

Believe it or not, starches, in and of themselves, are not the devil. Hear me out on this one.

There's a case to be made for starches. But first I think we need to get our heads on straight about carbohydrates in general. There seems to be a lot of confusion. In fact, when we say "carbs are evil!" most times we are speaking (erroneously) about starches and not about carbohydrates as a whole.

Carbohydrates, as a general category, encompass many different kinds of food. Fruits are carbohydrates. Vegetables are carbohydrates as well. Milk and beans? Also primarily sources of carbohydrates! So which ones are "good" and which are "bad"?

In my humble opinion there is no starch that is good or bad because starch is a food, not a person, and therefore cannot do anything to be good or bad.

Instead, there are starches that are healthy and starches that less healthy. Let's talk about those. Starches we tend to think of as the healthiest are "whole grain" starches. Whole grain means just that, the entire grain (be it wheat, barley, rice, etc.) was used in the production of the food. Whole grain foods tend to have higher fiber counts than their refined counterparts and more of the naturally occurring nutrients that are lost in the refinement process (although sometimes they are added back in to white starches from other sources).

Starches we consider the least healthy are refined starches. Those are things like white flour, white sugar, packaged starches like cakes, cookies, donuts and the like. I'm not going to go into a total breakdown of why these foods are less healthy for you (for that, if I were you, I'd talk to your registered dietician!) but I will say that many people overgeneralize the negative health effects of starches, and carbohydrates in general, when really they are thinking of this very small subset of starches.

That's a fancy way of saying carbs in general are not the devil, starches are not the devil, however, there are some unhealthy carbohydrates, including unhealthy starches. You still with me? Good!

I bring all of this up because when you are looking through this book you'll see recipes for pancakes. You'll see oatmeal. You'll see recipes that include cereal. I try to give advice where I can on picking a healthful starch. And there is merit in picking healthful starches. A good, healthful grain has lots of nutrients like iron, magnesium, selenium and B-vitamins. (Source: The Whole Grain Council)

And then there's the matter of fiber. Fiber has a few good purposes in your body. It acts like a scrub brush, cleaning out your innards and that helps you to have a healthy bathroom life (corny, but this is a food book so I'm trying to keep the graphic language down!). Diets with adequate fiber can also be heart-healthier and fiber can keep you satisfied longer. This may not be an issue for newer post-ops but trust me when I say it may very well be an issue a few years down the line.

The most important thing I want you to understand about fiber is this: fiber is found in carbohydrates. You cannot get fiber without consuming carbohydrates. Fiber supplements are mostly, if not all, fiber, which the human body doesn't absorb, but even then you are still consuming a carbohydrate. That's important to remember when you think about how carbohydrates will be a part of your life. For myself I do not say I will never eat carbohydrates, but that I will eat beneficial ones!

In the end, the decision is yours. In all things, I say again, defer to your bariatric program! If you've been advised to only eat certain kinds of carbohydrates or starches, do what your program says. If you've been told not to introduce certain foods until certain times, do what your program says. Bottom line: your bariatric program's advice always trumps mine!

Yogurt

When a post-op, do as the Greeks do?

Or maybe not. Greek yogurt is all the rage these days. And it's no wonder. Ounce for ounce, it has a higher protein count than its traditional counterpart and maintains a creamy texture even when it is low-fat or fat-free!

But what, exactly, *is* Greek yogurt?

The simplest explanation is that it is yogurt that has had the excess liquid strained from it, yielding a thick, creamy yogurt that, when unflavored, resembles sour cream in taste.

So should you eat Greek yogurt or regular yogurt?

There's no right or wrong answer. Most folks go with what they like best. I know some post-ops who are crazy about Greek yogurt (present company included) while others can't stand it no matter how you make it!

Whether you go with Greek or regular, know that yogurt has some great benefits. It's a great source of calcium and it has live, active cultures that help your body out in many ways (which I will not list because this is a food book).

If you do want to give Greek yogurt a try, three pieces of advice:

1. If you buy unflavored, it's going to taste sort of like sour cream. You have to add stuff to it to flavor it.
2. Watch the labels! The pre-flavored kinds can be laden with sugar as can the ones with fruit on the bottom. Greek yogurt, by virtue of the fact that it is a milk product, will have some sugar but most with no added sugar should have about 8-9g of milk sugar in a whole container.
3. Use it for other stuff besides fruit & yogurt! You can make ranch or French onion dips with Greek yogurt and you can also use it as sour cream (since the unflavored variety already tastes like it).

Meat

What kind of bacon should I eat?

I get this question a lot.

In the end, any food choice you make is yours alone. With regards to breakfast meat, most people want to know if the fat in pork products will deter their weight loss. I will say this many times in this, and other, Bariatric Foodie books. I'm not a registered dietician. I've certainly never played one on television. I cook. So my answer would be from a cooking perspective, which I think is still helpful as you and *your registered dietician* decide what's right for you.

Here's what I can say about breakfast meats:

1. **Fat = flavor.** The less fat there is in a breakfast meat, the more work the manufacturer of the meat had to do to create flavor. You may or may not be comfortable with how they did that (via added chemicals and/or sugar). Talk with your registered dietician about

how to read food labels so you can know what's in the food you're eating!

2. **Fat preserves moisture.** That's not to say there aren't other methods of preserving moisture in food. There are! But meat that is low in fat may need some help being moist. For a post-op this is of particular importance because dry food is food that is more likely to make you ill!

3. **Fat (along with other things) causes fullness.** This can be a good or a bad thing with regards to breakfast meat. If you overeat breakfast meat with a lot of fat, you run the risk of not feeling so great (I speak from experience). You also run the risk of filling up before you've gotten the proper amount of nutrients and protein.

While I can't give you nutritional advice, I usually err on the side of consuming a combination of low-fat and regular-fat breakfast meats. I've also seen people:

1. Only eat low-fat, non-pork bacon, like turkey or soy bacon, and never eat pork bacon.
2. Only eat pork bacon, just not very often.
3. Eat mostly turkey or other low-fat bacon but sometimes eat pork bacon.

I am camp #3. I like turkey bacon, but don't eat it often. I don't eat bacon in general very often because I know I like the pork! Your decision? Totally yours. However, my recipes all work with either pork or turkey bacon.

Chapter Two:
Fun with Eggs

In this chapter, we'll talk even more about eggs, the quintessential breakfast food! And of course, there are also lots of egg recipes.

A few notes about the recipes in this book:

- For many recipes, you'll see two versions. The "smaller" version is ideal for people who have a lot of restriction and eat very small portions. The "full version" is ideal for people who have a bit more eating capacity. PLEASE NOTE: There are no connotations here. If you use the full version, that does not mean you are a glutton, eating too much or anything else your brain wants to tell you. As time goes on you are supposed to be able to eat more and the full version of these recipes is still a vastly smaller meal than you would have eaten pre-op. So no mind games! Fix whichever version is right for you!
- One thing you will NOT find in most of my recipes is nutrition information. There's a reason for that. Because the nutrition information in the products available to each of us varies so much, and because there is a natural tendency to modify recipes, I refrain from putting this information on my recipes. Instead, at the end of this book, I explain how you can figure out the nutrition information in the dish, as you made it.
- However, rest assured recipes are written to have a sensible amount of calories, fat and carbohydrates, while getting the most protein possible.
- There are no pictures of food in this book. That has more to do with cost than anything else. Pictures are best printed in color, color is more expensive to print and if I had to pay more to print in color, I would have to pass those costs on to you in the price of the book. I strive to make the price of these books reasonable and so I'm sorry but no pictures!

With that information in hand, let us journey forward!

The Challenge of Eggs in a Post-Op Life

Eggs are an iconic breakfast food. Whether you like yours sunny side up, over-easy, scrambled or poached, for some people breakfast just isn't breakfast without eggs!

In this section you'll find my best advice for incorporating eggs into your cooking as well as yummy egg recipes!

So let's get started, shall we?

But first...can you tolerate an egg?

Many post-ops can't. I don't know why. Truth be told, I don't think science knows why either. There is a list of things that tend to make post-ops ill or uncomfortable that seems to be a mystery (like plain water for some post ops). I'm sorry I don't have a better explanation for you but I point this out to say that if you're new and have never tried eggs before, there is a chance you may not tolerate them. I tolerated them fine. So there's also a chance that you will too!

Egg texture: Why it's important

You probably already know a lot about the texture of eggs, at least with regards to how you liked them before surgery. When you sit down to order eggs in a restaurant, some of you will ask for an egg to be fried hard. Some of you love "fluffy" scrambled eggs.

The texture of a cooked egg has a lot to do with the preparation of the raw egg. In general, if you don't introduce much air to an egg in its raw state and cook it very fast and on high heat, you'll come out with a firmer egg. If you introduce a lot of air to an egg in the raw state (usually by way of "beating" or "whipping" the egg) you come out with a softer egg. Some people add milk and other things to eggs to soften them but it really does come down to the handling of the egg before you cook it.

Having said that, when I was a new post op I found this basic scrambled egg recipe to be very "me-friendly" and, as a bonus, it has added protein!

Nik's Newbie-friendly Scrambled Eggs
- 1 egg
- 2 tablespoons cottage cheese
- Seasonings to taste (I like a little salt and pepper, but that's about it)

Whip eggs vigorously for a full minute (until the entire mixture is yellow and bubbly). Add cottage cheese and spices and mix again.

Set a pan over medium heat and allow it to get hot, but not smoking. Spray with non-stick cooking spray and add the egg mixture. Gently stir with a wooden spoon until completely done (this will take longer than regular scrambled eggs).

I'll warn you, these aren't the prettiest eggs you've ever seen but they are easier on the stomach and they have a little bit more protein because of the cottage cheese!

Eggs: Do they reheat well?

It's a toss-up and, again, comes back to how they are prepared.

I hear from a lot of people who have had problems reheating scrambled eggs. I'm not sure if this has much to do with the eggs themselves or what we tend to put *in* eggs. Many of us eat scrambled eggs with shredded cheese. Shredded cheese has been produced to hold its form, which sometimes makes it harder to digest when reheated. Some vegetables and meats also toughen and/or dry out when reheating. Eggs themselves are a pretty firm protein when cooked and thus can be hard to eat reheated.

From what I've heard from others, along with my personal experience, the above egg scramble does well with reheating. You'll also find mini-frittata recipes in this section that have always reheated well for me. As with all things, you may have a different experience! I'd say if reheated eggs normally make you ill, you should experiment some with these recipes before trying to consume them outside your home. Sound fair? Good!

Now...on to the other recipes!

Scrambles

In my experience egg scrambles can be a great way to have the taste of foods that are *really* not great for you. For instance, on the pages that follow you'll find a Reuben scramble and a Cheesesteak scramble (*steak* not cake!).

While the recipes in this section are all tailored to an individual portion, you can easily make them family style by making the following changes. These changes apply to all the scramble recipes, regardless of what the scramble contains.

How to make my scrambles work for a family of four:

- Use six eggs or one cup liquid egg substitute.
- Where a recipe calls for diced onion, use a whole small onion.
- Where a recipe calls for diced green pepper, use a whole small green pepper.
- Use at least six ounces of protein (like chicken, beef, shrimp, etc. Some of the recipes below call for several kinds of proteins. You can decide how much of each you want to use to make up that six ounces!)
- When using pepperoni, use two servings (check the nutrition label for serving sizes).
- If using shredded cheese, use ¾ cup. If using Laughing Cow Light wedges, use four.
- Adjust the spices as you see fit, but for anything with a kick I recommend you use no more than ¼ tablespoon unless you know everyone likes spicy food!

For you, one portion of a scramble will be enough to make a meal. For the family, I'd serve with toast, a biscuit, fruit salad or maybe even pancakes!

Cheesesteak Scramble[*]
(That's CheeseSTEAK, not cake!)

Smaller version:

- 1 tbsp. finely chopped onion
- 1 tbsp. finely chopped green pepper
- 1-2 slices thin, low-sodium deli roast beef, roughly chopped
- 1 egg, beaten OR ¼ c. liquid egg substitute
- ½ thin slice provolone cheese, cut into pieces OR a Laughing Cow Light French Onion cheese wedge
- Salt and pepper, to taste
- Optional topping: low-sugar ketchup

Full version:

- 2 tbsp. chopped onion
- 1 tbsp. chopped green pepper
- 2-3 slices low-sodium deli-roast beef (sliced to desired thickness), rough chopped
- 1 egg + 1 egg white (or 2 whole eggs OR 3 whole egg whites), beaten OR ½ c. liquid egg substitute
- ½ slice provolone cheese, cut into pieces OR a Laughing Cow Light French Onion cheese wedge
- Salt and pepper, to taste
- Optional topping: low-sugar ketchup

Directions:

Spray a skillet with nonstick cooking spray, set it over medium heat and allow the pan to get hot (one to two minutes).

Add onion and green pepper and sauté about a minute before adding chopped roast beef.

Cook beef/vegetable mixture until beef has slightly crisped (if you desire, you can cook it further to achieve even crispier meat).

Spread the mixture around the pan and add eggs and cheese. Gently stir mixture until it is cooked thoroughly. Transfer to a plate and top with any desired toppings.

Spot Check: Low-fat soft cheese wedges rarely just melt into dishes as they cook. It may be necessary to cut it into pieces or pre-mix it into your eggs.

---

[*] My Version has _____ calories, _____ total carbohydrates, _____ fiber, _____ sugar, _____ protein

Reuben Scramble*

Smaller version:

- 1 tbsp. finely chopped onion
- ½ slice corned beef OR pastrami, chopped into small pieces
- 1 egg, beaten OR ¼ c. liquid egg substitute
- 1 wedge Laughing Cow Light Swiss cheese
- A pinch of caraway seed
- 1 tbsp. prepared sauerkraut (NOTE: This is a great way to use leftovers!)
- 1 tbsp. low-calorie 1000 Island OR Russian dressing

Full version:

- 2 tbsp. chopped onion
- 1 slice corned beef OR pastrami, chopped into small pieces
- 1 egg + 1 egg white (or 2 whole eggs or 3 egg whites), beaten OR ½ c. liquid egg substitute
- 1 wedge Laughing Cow Light Swiss cheese
- A pinch of caraway seed
- 1 tbsp. prepared sauerkraut
- 1 tbsp. low calorie 1000 Island OR Russian dressing

Directions:

Spray a skillet with nonstick cooking spray, set it over medium heat and allow the pan to get hot (one to two minutes).

Add onion and sauté about a minute before adding meat.

Cook meat/vegetable mixture until beef has slightly crisped (if you desire, you can cook it further to achieve even crispier meat).

Spread the mixture around the pan and add eggs, caraway seed, cheese and sauerkraut. Gently stir mixture until it is cooked thoroughly. Transfer to a plate and top with dressing.

Spot Check: Low-fat soft cheese wedges rarely just melt into dishes as they cook. It may be necessary to cut it into pieces or pre-mix it into your eggs.

---

* My Version has _____ calories, _____ total carbohydrates, _____ fiber, _____ sugar, _____ protein

Mexican Scramble[*]

Smaller version:

- 1 tbsp. finely chopped onion
- 1 tbsp. finely chopped green pepper
- 1 oz. chorizo sausage, casing removed
- 1 egg, beaten OR ¼ c. liquid egg substitute
- 2 tbsp. Mexican blend cheese
- Salt and pepper, to taste
- Optional: (For egg mixture) Sliced jalapeno peppers, sliced black olives. (For topping) Salsa, unflavored Greek yogurt

Full version:

- 2 tbsp. chopped onion
- 2 tbsp. chopped green pepper
- 2 oz. chorizo sausage, casing removed
- 1 egg + 1 egg white (or 2 whole eggs OR 3 whole egg whites), beaten OR ½ c. liquid egg substitute
- ¼ c. Mexican blend cheese
- Optional: (For egg mixture) Sliced jalapeno peppers, sliced black olives. (For topping) Salsa, unflavored Greek yogurt

Directions:

Spray a skillet with nonstick cooking spray, set it over medium heat and allow the pan to get hot (one to two minutes).

Add onion and green pepper and sauté about a minute before adding chopped chorizo sausage.

Brown the chorizo sausage like you would ground beef (making sure to chop it into tiny pieces) and cook until completely done through.

Spread mixture around the pan before adding the eggs and cheese. If you are using optional mix-ins, add them at this point.

Gently stir with a wooden spoon until fully cooked. Transfer to a plate and top with desired toppings.

Spot Check: Chorizo sausage comes in many varieties — from low-fat versions like chicken or turkey to traditional pork. Choose which one is right for you!

---

* My Version has _____ calories, _____ total carbohydrates, _____ fiber, _____ sugar, _____ protein

17

Farmer's Scramble[*]

NOTE: You should be cleared to eat cooked vegetables before consuming this scramble!

Smaller version:

- 1 tbsp. finely chopped onion
- 1 tbsp. finely chopped green pepper
- 1 button mushroom, chopped into pieces of desired size
- About 10 leaves baby spinach
- A few shakes of garlic powder OR 1/8 tsp. minced garlic
- 1 egg, beaten OR ¼ c. liquid egg substitute
- 1 Laughing Cow Light cheese wedge, in any flavor you like
- Salt and pepper, to taste

Full version:

- 2 tbsp. finely chopped onion
- 2 tbsp. finely chopped green pepper
- 1-2 button mushrooms, chopped into pieces of desired size
- ½ c. baby spinach
- A few shakes of garlic powder OR ¼ tsp. minced garlic
- 1 egg + 1 egg white (or 2 whole eggs OR 3 whole egg whites), beaten OR ½ c. liquid egg substitute
- 1 Laughing Cow Light cheese wedge, in any flavor you like
- Salt and pepper, to taste

Directions:

Spray a skillet with nonstick cooking spray, set it over medium heat and allow the pan to get hot (one to two minutes).

Add all vegetables and sauté for two to three minutes, or until soft and spinach is wilted. Add garlic and sauté a moment longer.

Spread veggie mixture around the pan a bit and add egg and cheese. Gently turn mixture with a wooden spoon until eggs, veggies and cheese are all mixed and eggs are thoroughly cooked.

Transfer to a plate.

Spot Check: Low-fat soft cheese wedges rarely just melt into dishes as they cook. It may be necessary to cut it into pieces or pre-mix it into your eggs.

---

* My Version has _____ calories, _____ total carbohydrates, _____ fiber, _____ sugar, _____ protein

Pizza Scramble*

Smaller version:

- 1 tbsp. finely chopped onion
- 1 tbsp. finely chopped green peppers
- 1 egg, beaten, OR ¼ c. liquid egg substitute
- 1/8 tsp. Italian seasoning
- Choose one of the following: 6 slices turkey pepperoni OR 1 tablespoon sausage crumbles
- 2 tbsp. low-sugar pizza OR spaghetti sauce, warmed
- 2 tbsp. shredded part-skim mozzarella cheese

Full version:

- 2 tbsp. chopped onion
- 2 tbsp. chopped green peppers
- 1/8 tsp. Italian seasoning
- 1 egg + 1 egg white (or 2 whole eggs OR 3 egg whites), beaten OR ½ c. liquid egg substitute
- Choose one of the following: 10 slices turkey pepperoni OR ¼ c. sausage crumbles
- ¼ c. low-sugar pizza OR spaghetti sauce, warmed
- 2 tbsp. shredded part-skim mozzarella cheese

Optional: (For topping)

- Sliced black olives, red pepper flakes, grated Parmesan cheese

Directions:

Spray a skillet with nonstick cooking spray, set it over medium heat and allow it to get hot.

Add vegetables and sauté for one to two minutes or until soft.

Add eggs and seasoning and stir gently with a wooden spoon until cooked through.

Transfer to a plate and quickly top with warmed sauce and shredded cheese, allowing the hot eggs to melt the cheese. Add any additional desired toppings.

---

* My Version has _____ calories, _____ total carbohydrates, _____ fiber, _____ sugar, _____ protein

Greek Scramble[*]

Smaller version:

- 1 egg, beaten OR ¼ c. liquid egg substitute
- 1/8 tsp. Greek seasoning
- 1 tbsp. finely chopped red onions
- 1 tbsp. sliced Kalamata olives
- 1 tbsp. petite diced tomatoes
- ½ oz. feta cheese OR 1 Laughing Cow Light Feta wedge

Full version:

- 1 egg + 1 egg white (or 2 whole eggs or 3 egg whites), beaten OR ½ c. liquid egg substitute
- 1/8 tsp. Greek seasoning
- 2 tbsp. chopped red onions
- 2 tbsp. sliced Kalamata olives
- 1-2 tbsp. petite diced tomatoes
- ½ oz. Feta cheese OR 1 Laughing Cow Light Feta wedge
- Optional: (For topping: Cold, diced cucumber and unflavored Greek yogurt)

Directions:

Spray a skillet with nonstick cooking spray, set it over medium heat and allow it to get hot.

In a bowl, mix together eggs, Greek seasoning and Feta cheese.

Transfer to pan and stir with a wooden spoon until eggs are almost fully cooked.

Add olives, tomatoes and onions and stir to mix through and finish cooking.

Spot Check: If you don't like a strong onion flavor, sauté the red onions in the skillet 1-2 minutes before adding the egg mixture. This will tone down the onion flavor.

Transfer to a plate and add desired toppings.

Spot Check: Low-fat soft cheese wedges rarely just melt into dishes as they cook. It may be necessary to cut it into pieces.

---

[*] My Version has _____ calories, _____ total carbohydrates, _____ fiber, _____ sugar, _____ protein

Meat Lovers Scramble*

Smaller version:

- 1 tbsp. finely chopped onions
- 1 tbsp. sausage crumbles
- ½ tbsp. bacon bits
- 4-5 turkey pepperoni
- 1 egg, beaten, OR ¼ c. liquid egg substitute
- 1 wedge Laughing Cow Light cheese in your flavor of choice

Full version:

- 2 tbsp. finely diced onions
- 2 tbsp. sausage crumbles
- 1 tbsp. bacon bits
- 4-5 turkey pepperoni
- 1 egg + 1 egg white (or 2 whole eggs OR 3 egg whites), beaten OR ½ c. liquid egg substitute
- 1 wedge Laughing Cow Light cheese in your flavor of choice

Directions:

Spray a skillet down with nonstick cooking spray, set it over medium heat and allow it to get hot.

Add onion and sauté for one minute.

Add sausage crumbles, bacon bits and pepperoni and allow them to get to desired crispiness.

Add egg and cheese and gently stir with a fork until eggs are completely done and cheese is distributed and melted throughout.

Spot Check: Low-fat soft cheese wedges rarely just melt into dishes as they cook. It may be necessary to cut it into pieces or pre-mix it into your eggs.

---

* My Version has _____ calories, _____ total carbohydrates, _____ fiber, _____ sugar, _____ protein

Seafood Scramble[*]

Smaller version:

- 1 tbsp. finely diced onion
- ½ oz. baby shrimp (from a can)
- ½ oz. imitation or real crab meat OR ½ oz. soft white fish, like tilapia, cooked (NOTE: This is a great way to use leftovers!)
- 1 egg, beaten, OR ¼ c. liquid egg substitute
- 1 wedge Laughing Cow Light French Onion OR 1 tbsp. low-fat cream cheese
- 1/8 tsp. seafood seasoning

Full version:

- 2 tbsp. finely diced onion
- 2 tbsp. baby shrimp (from a can)
- 2 tbsp. imitation or real crab meat OR 1 oz. soft white fish, like tilapia, cooked (NOTE: This is a great way to use leftovers!)
- 1 egg + 1 egg white (or 2 whole eggs or 3 egg whites), beaten OR ½ c. liquid egg substitute
- 1 wedge Laughing Cow Light French Onion OR 1 tbsp. low-fat cream cheese
- 1/8 tsp. seafood seasoning

Directions:

Spray a skillet down with nonstick cooking spray, set it over medium heat and allow it to get hot.

Add onion and sauté for one minute.

Add seafood and sauté an additional two minutes

Add egg, cheese and seasoning and gently stir with a fork until eggs are completely done and cheese is distributed and melted throughout.

Spot Check: Low-fat soft cheese wedges rarely just melt into dishes as they cook. It may be necessary to cut it into pieces or pre-mix it into your eggs.

---

[*] My Version has _____ calories, _____ total carbohydrates, _____ fiber, _____ sugar, _____ protein

Egg Casseroles & Other Quiche-y Things

The ideas in this section all started with concept of a crustless quiche which is, simply put, a quiche without a crust! They can be made in a pie plate for a family style quiche or a muffin or mini-muffin tin for easy grab-and-go meals.

An **egg casserole** is like a crustless quiche, except heartier. It's not as light as a quiche. It's got some weight! Just a small slice of one of my egg casseroles is enough to fill up most post-ops but it has enough protein for just that small piece to be enough! At the same time, a larger slice is completely satisfying to a "non-op" (person who has not had bariatric surgery). Another distinction of an egg casserole is that it can be served for lunch or dinner and it doesn't read like "breakfast for dinner."

But I know some of you are just cooking for one OR you are the only one eating weight loss surgery friendly food! No worries. Any of my Egg Casserole/"Quiche-y" recipes easily convert into more freeze-able forms like mini-egg muffins (sometimes called mini-crustless quiches).

In general, **the recipes in this section convert to approximately 24 mini-egg muffins**, although your yield may vary based on the size of your pan. If that's too many for you (although they do freeze well when properly wrapped), try halving the recipe.

With that information in hand, let's explore the wonderful world of egg casseroles…and other "quiche-y" things!

Mexican Egg Casserole[*]

Ingredients:

- 1 small onion, finely diced
- 1 small green pepper, finely diced
- 8 oz. can mild tomatoes & chilies
- 8 oz. chorizo sausage (get mild if you don't like spicy food)
- 10 oz. can of beans (or you can use a mixture of beans amounting to that much, like red kidney and black beans), drained
- 1 c. shredded Mexican blend cheese, divided
- ½ c. milk
- 6 eggs (or the equivalent amount of liquid egg substitute)
- A pinch each: salt, pepper, cumin, coriander
- Optional additions (to make a spicier casserole):
  2 Serrano peppers, finely diced, seeds included (NOTE: wear gloves to protect your hands)
  A generous dash of cayenne pepper (OR if you like it really hot, ground chipotle powder)

Directions:

Preheat your oven to 350 degrees.

Spray a skillet with nonstick cooking spray and toss in your onions, green and serrano peppers. Let them cook until tender.

Cut your chorizo sausage out of the casing and add to pan. Brown it as you would ground beef. Add tomatoes and chiles and warm through.

In a large bowl, mix eggs with milk and seasonings. Add ½ cup of cheese and beat again.

Spread meat/veggie mixture out in a 9 inch x 13 inch casserole dish.

Pour egg mixture on top and stir it into the meat mixture with a wooden spoon. Top with remaining cheese.

Bake at 350 degrees for 30 minutes or until completely cooked and cheese is slightly browned.

Set on a cooling rack for five to 10 minutes before slicing into pieces of desired size.

Spot Check: Chorizo sausage comes in many varieties. If you are watching calories, look for reduced-fat turkey or chicken varieties.

---

[*] My Version has _____ calories, _____ total carbohydrates, _____ fiber, _____ sugar, _____ protein

Crab-Asiago Egg Casserole[*]

Ingredients:

- 8 oz. real or imitation crab meat
- 1 small onion, diced
- 1 large tomato, diced
- 1 small green pepper, finely diced
- 6 eggs, beaten (or equivalent amount of liquid egg substitute)
- 1 cup shredded Asiago cheese
- ½ cup shredded part-skim mozzarella
- ½ cup shredded Parmesan cheese
- Salt and pepper, to taste

Directions:

Preheat your oven to 350 degrees.

Empty crab meat into a large mixing bowl and sift through to pick out any remaining shells.

Add veggies and mix thoroughly.

In a separate bowl, whisk together milk, eggs and all three cheeses, salt and pepper.

Transfer crab meat/veggie mixture to a 8 inch x 8 inch casserole dish and spread it evenly.

Pour egg/cheese mixture onto the crab mixture and stir with a wooden spoon to combine.

Bake at 350 degrees for 30 minutes or until completely cooked.

Transfer to a cooling rack for five to 10 minutes before cutting into slices of desired size.

Spot Check: You don't have to cook the veggies before adding them to the crab mixture, but if the texture of vegetables sometimes bothers you, you may want to sauté the veggies in a pan sprayed with nonstick cooking spray for one to two minutes before adding to the crab.

---

* My Version has _____ calories, _____ total carbohydrates, _____ fiber, _____ sugar, _____ protein

Cajun Egg Casserole[*]

Ingredients:

- 8 oz. Andouille sausage, casings removed
- 1 small onion, finely diced
- 1 small green pepper, finely diced
- 2 c. baby spinach (OR if you want to be really authentic, try a cup of sliced okra!)
- 1 clove garlic, minced
- 8 oz. can tomatoes and chilies
- 1 c. shredded Pepper Jack cheese, divided
- ½ c. milk
- 6 eggs (or the equivalent amount of liquid egg substitute)
- ¼ tsp. Cajun seasoning
- Salt and pepper, to taste
- Optional: 1 jalapeno pepper, seeded and diced

Directions:

Preheat your oven to 350 degrees.

Spray a skillet with nonstick cooking spray, set it over medium heat and allow it to get hot. Add sausage and break up into small pieces, as if browning ground meat. Cook two to three minutes.

Add onion, green pepper, spinach and garlic and mix into meat. Cook until vegetables have softened and spinach is wilted.

In a separate bowl, combine eggs, milk, cheese and spices. Whisk until eggs are slightly bubbly.

If necessary, drain meat/veggie mixture of excess fat in a colander and then transfer to a 9 inch x 13 inch casserole dish. Spread mixture around dish, then pour egg/cheese mixture in, stirring the entire mixture with a wooden spoon to combine.

Bake at 350 degrees for 30 minutes or until completely cooked. Transfer to a cooling rack for five to 10 minutes before cutting into slices of desired size.

Spot Check: You can get even more protein into this dish by adding diced chicken and baby shrimp for a jambalaya spin!

---

* My Version has _____ calories, _____ total carbohydrates, _____ fiber, _____ sugar, _____ protein

Spinach & Bacon Quiche[*]

Ingredients:

- 6 eggs (or equivalent amount of liquid egg substitute)
- ¼ cup 0% fat Greek Yogurt
- 1 tbsp. garlic powder
- 1 tbsp. onion powder
- ¼ c. 2% milk
- 1 ½ c. spinach dip OR creamed spinach (look in the freezer section of the grocery store OR this is a great way to use leftovers!)
- 1 cup shredded Italian blend cheese
- ¾ jar of Hormel Real Bacon Bits (or 2 slices bacon, cooked and chopped)
- 1 small pat butter
- 1 tsp. olive oil
- Salt and pepper to taste

Directions:

Preheat oven to 400 degrees.

In a mixing bowl, combine eggs, milk, yogurt, bacon, half of the cheese and seasonings. Beat mixture until eggs are slightly frothy and there are no visible lumps.

Spray an oven-safe skillet with nonstick cooking spray, set it over medium heat and allow it to get hot. Add creamed spinach and stir until heated through.

Add eggs and bacon bits and stir with a rubber spatula until combined. Cook until eggs are about 2/3 done but still in a solid mass (like an omelet). Sprinkle the remaining cheese evenly over the top.

Bake in the oven for eight to 10 minutes or until the top is done and the cheese is thoroughly melted. Cool on a cooling rack before cutting into slices of desired size.

Spot Check: Your oven-safe skillet should be safe up to at least 400 degrees. Also, if you want to cut calories you can use turkey bacon and crumble it yourself!

---

* My Version has _____ calories, _____ total carbohydrates, _____ fiber, _____ sugar, _____ protein

Caramelized Onion Quiche*

Ingredients:

- 1 tbsp. butter (or butter substitute but it should be appropriate for pan cooking)
- 1 large Vidalia onion, sliced into thin rings
- 1 tsp. minced garlic
- 1 c. Dill Havarti, shredded
- ½ c. milk
- 1 tsp. baking soda
- 6 eggs (or equivalent amount of liquid egg substitute)

Directions:

Preheat your oven to 350 degrees.

Melt butter in a nonstick skillet over medium heat. Add onion.

Drop the heat to medium-low and cook onions, stirring constantly, about 10 minutes or until they are brown in color and cooked soft.

Spot Check: If onions absorb all your butter, spray them with nonstick cooking spray to keep them cooking until they are caramelized.

Add garlic and stir. Meanwhile in a separate bowl, whisk together eggs and baking soda, then add milk and cheese until eggs are slightly frothy.

Add onions to a 9 inch x 13 inch casserole dish. Pour egg/cheese mixture on top and stir with a wooden spoon until combined.

Bake at 350 degrees for 30 minutes or until completely done through. Cool on a cooling rack before cutting into slices of desired size.

---

* My Version has _____ calories, _____ total carbohydrates, _____ fiber, _____ sugar, _____ protein

"Steak" & Mushroom Quiche[*]

Ingredients:

- 1 small onion, diced
- 1 small green pepper, diced
- 6 button mushrooms, sliced
- 8 oz. thin sliced, low-sodium deli roast beef, chopped up
- 6 eggs (or equivalent amount of liquid egg substitute)
- 1 cup shredded provolone cheese (or any mild cheese of your choosing)
- ½ c. milk
- 1 tsp. baking soda

Directions:

Preheat your oven to 350 degrees.

Spray a skillet with nonstick cooking spray, set it over medium heat and allow it to get hot.

Add onion, green pepper and mushrooms and sauté about two to three minutes, until green peppers and onions are slightly softened.

Add meat, stir and cook until meat has reached desired level of doneness.

In a separate bowl, whisk together eggs and baking soda, then add cheese and whisk until eggs are slightly frothy.

Transfer beef/veggie mixture to a 9 inch x 13 inch casserole dish and pour egg/cheese mixture over it. Use a wooden spoon to thoroughly combine everything.

Bake at 350 degrees for 30 minutes or until completely done. Cool on a cooling rack before cutting into slices of desired size.

---

* My Version has _____ calories, _____ total carbohydrates, _____ fiber, _____ sugar, _____ protein

Mini Frittatas

Ok, so first, what the heck is a frittata?

The answer is, depends on who you ask!

Originally frittatas were an Italian dish. The "fritta" in frittata means "to fry" as eggs are so often done. In researching this book, I found that some people think of frittatas as pan fried quiches. That's not exactly how I have experienced them, so I'll give you my interpretation.

Frittatas are like big ol' egg pancakes with really good stuff in them. What makes them special is that you start cooking them in a pan and then finish them in the oven. This allows the frittata to puff up slightly, finish cooking gently and, in my experience, yields a kinder, gentler egg!

The great thing about the frittata ideas in this section is that a lot of them call for things you might have left over from other meals. Many weight loss surgery post-ops worry about wasting leftovers. Don't waste leftovers, repurpose them into this elegant looking (and tasting) breakfast!

You'll need a few special supplies to make a bariatric-friendly frittata:

1. A 7 and 1/8 inch (yes that is the measurement) oven-safe skillet. Your skillet should be safe up to 500 degrees.
2. A rubber spatula (like the kind you use to scrape gooey cookie batter from a batter bowl! Sorry…but I bet you have the image in your head now, don't you?)
3. This should go without saying, but a good set of oven mitts! You would not believe how many times I have tried to extract oven-safe skillets from the oven without a mitt. I'm so used to being able to touch the handle!

Each of these frittata recipes yields a very small frittata. The recipes call for only one egg and a tiny bit of extra "stuff." Still, for some of you, this will still be a lot of food! If so, you can slice your frittata into wedges, wrap tightly in plastic wrap, then place them in a freezer safe bag. They keep well in the freezer for up to a month. To reheat, first let them thaw, then microwave. NOTE: Be careful about microwaving eggs (especially eggs with cheese) if you are new. It may bother your new anatomy!

Fiesta Chicken Frittata[*]

Ingredients:

- 1 oz. diced chicken (great way to use up leftovers!)
- 1 egg, beaten (or equivalent amount of liquid egg substitute)
- A pinch of baking soda
- 2 tbsp. prepared salsa
- 2 tbsp. shredded Mexican-blend cheese
- ¼ tsp. taco seasoning (OR a pinch each of ground cumin, coriander, chili powder and cayenne pepper)
- Optional: Unflavored Greek yogurt (for topping), additional salsa

Directions:

Preheat your oven to 350 degrees.

Spray a 7 and 1/8 inch oven-safe skillet generously with nonstick cooking spray, set it over a medium flame and let it get hot.

Add diced chicken to warm through. Meanwhile, in a bowl whisk together eggs and baking soda and then combine with spices, salsa and half the cheese.

Spot Check: The baking soda in this and other egg recipes is used as a leavening agent to make the eggs "puff up." It helps them maintain a softer texture than the eggs alone would have. Besides baking soda, you can also use either baking powder or cream of tartar. Some people report a metallic taste with baking soda (I've never noticed it). Alternatively, to soften your eggs you could use a bit more fat in the form of a tablespoon of half and half.

Pour egg mixture over chicken and swirl the pan lightly to coat with the egg mixture (it should be a circle of egg). Use a rubber spatula to gently stir the contents to distribute them evenly around the pan.

Cook on stove until edges are set, gently running the spatula under the edges to ensure they don't stick.

Top with additional cheese and bake in the oven for seven to 10 minutes or until completely done and cheese is browned.

Spot Check: Upon extracting from the oven, the frittata should come out of the pan easily. If it doesn't automatically slide out, run the spatula beneath it, then gently transfer it to a plate. You can also cut it into small wedges for better portioning.

---

[*] My Version has _____ calories, _____ total carbohydrates, _____ fiber, _____ sugar, _____ protein

Pizza Frittata[*]

Ingredients:

- 1 tbsp. onion, diced very small
- 1 tbsp. green pepper, diced very small
- 1 egg, beaten (or equivalent amount of liquid egg substitute)
- A pinch of baking soda
- 2 tbsp. either shredded mozzarella OR Italian blend cheese
- 6-8 turkey pepperonis

Directions:

Preheat your oven to 350 degrees.

Spray a 7 and 1/8 inch oven-safe skillet generously with nonstick cooking spray, set it over a medium flame and let it get hot.

Add onions and green pepper and sauté about one minute. Meanwhile, in a bowl whisk together eggs and baking soda and then combine with half the cheese.

Spot Check: The baking soda in this and other egg recipes is used as a leavening agent to make the eggs "puff up." It helps them maintain a softer texture than the eggs alone would have. Besides baking soda, you can also use either baking powder or cream of tartar. Some people report a metallic taste with baking soda (I've never noticed it). Alternatively, to soften your eggs you could use a bit more fat in the form of a tablespoon of half and half.

Pour egg mixture over the veggies and swirl the pan lightly to coat with the egg mixture (it should be a circle of egg). Use a rubber spatula to gently stir the contents to distribute them evenly around the pan.

Cook on stove until edges are set, gently running the spatula under the edges to ensure they don't stick.

Top with additional cheese, then the pepperoni, and bake in the oven for seven to 10 minutes or until completely done and cheese is browned.

Spot Check: Upon extracting from the oven, the frittata should come out of the pan easily. If it doesn't automatically slide out, run the spatula beneath it, then gently transfer it to a plate. You can also cut it into small wedges for better portioning.

---

* My Version has _____ calories, _____ total carbohydrates, _____ fiber, _____ sugar, _____ protein

Denver Frittata[*]

Ingredients:

- 1 tbsp. onions, diced very small
- 1 tbsp. green peppers, diced very small
- 1 oz. ham, diced very small (great use for leftovers!)
- 1 egg, beaten (or equivalent amount of liquid egg substitute)
- A pinch of baking soda
- 2 tbsp. shredded cheddar cheese, divided

Directions:

Preheat your oven to 350 degrees.

Spray a 7 and 1/8 inch oven-safe skillet generously with nonstick cooking spray, set it over a medium flame and let it get hot.

Add onions, green pepper and ham and sauté about two minutes. Meanwhile, in a bowl whisk together eggs and baking soda and then combine with half the cheese.

Spot Check: The baking soda in this and other egg recipes is used as a leavening agent to make the eggs "puff up." It helps them maintain a softer texture than the eggs alone would have. Besides baking soda, you can also use either baking soda or cream of tartar. Some people report a metallic taste with baking soda (I've never noticed it). Alternatively, to soften your eggs you could use a bit more fat in the form of a tablespoon of half and half.

Pour egg mixture over the veggies and swirl the pan lightly to coat with the egg mixture (it should be a circle of egg). Use a rubber spatula to gently stir the contents to distribute them evenly around the pan.

Cook on stove until edges are set, gently running the spatula under the edges to ensure they don't stick.

Top with additional cheese and bake in the oven for seven to 10 minutes or until completely done and cheese is browned.

Spot Check: Upon extracting from the oven, the frittata should come out of the pan easily. If it doesn't automatically slide out, run the spatula beneath it, then gently transfer it to a plate. You can also cut it into small wedges for better portioning.

---

* My Version has _____ calories, _____ total carbohydrates, _____ fiber, _____ sugar, _____ protein

Hawaiian Frittata*

Ingredients:

- 1 tbsp. red onion, diced very small
- 1 tbsp. green pepper, diced very small
- 1 oz. ham, diced very small
- 1 egg, beaten (or equivalent amount liquid egg substitute)
- A pinch of baking soda
- 2 tbsp. shredded white cheddar cheese, divided
- 2 pineapple chunks, roughly chopped

Directions:

Preheat your oven to 350 degrees.

Spray a 7 and 1/8 inch oven-safe skillet generously with nonstick cooking spray, set it over a medium flame and let it get hot.

Add onions, green pepper and ham and sauté about two minutes. Meanwhile, in a bowl whisk together eggs and baking soda and then combine with pineapple and half the cheese.

Spot Check: The baking soda in this and other egg recipes is used as a leavening agent to make the eggs "puff up." It helps them maintain a softer texture than the eggs alone would have. Besides baking soda, you can also use either baking soda or cream of tartar. Some people report a metallic taste with baking soda (I've never noticed it). Alternatively, to soften your eggs you could use a bit more fat in the form of a tablespoon of half and half.

Pour egg mixture over the veggies and swirl the pan lightly to coat with the egg mixture (it should be a circle of egg). Use a rubber spatula to gently stir the contents to distribute them evenly around the pan.

Cook on stove until edges are set, gently running the spatula under the edges to ensure they don't stick.

Top with additional cheese and bake in the oven for seven to 10 minutes or until completely done and cheese is browned.

Spot Check: Upon extracting from the oven, the frittata should come out of the pan easily. If it doesn't automatically slide out, run the spatula beneath it, then gently transfer it to a plate. You can also cut it into small wedges for better portioning.

---

* My Version has _____ calories, _____ total carbohydrates, _____ fiber, _____ sugar, _____ protein

34

Other Unique Egg Dishes

Because eggs are one of my personal "safe foods" (aka food I can eat without the threat of getting deathly ill), I have experimented with them a lot.

Some of the dishes I've come up with are very…unique. They don't fit into any one category of egg dishes so I thought I'd give them their own section!

Think of these recipes as a template. You can substitute any of the vegetables I propose with veggies you like better (NOTE: Cruciferous veggies like broccoli and cauliflower take longer to cook, so cook those to al dente – not hard, not soft – before adding any other veggies or additions). You can also substitute any protein you like and, as we discussed at the beginning of the book, use whatever egg or egg-like product you want!

Since these are a little outside the box, I gave short explanations for them. I hope they help you embrace the goodness of experimentation!

Enjoy!

The Egg-chilada[*]

One day I was going to make scrambled eggs. I dumped my beaten eggs on my griddle pan and got a phone call, got engrossed and came back to find this huge "sheet" of egg. So I did what any sane person would do...I flipped it. Then once that side was cooked I looked at it and thought, "This looks like a gigantic tortilla. I wonder if I put stuff in it, if it'd look like an enchilada!"

And the Egg-chilada was born.

Ingredients:

- 1 egg, beaten (or equivalent amount of liquid egg substitute)
- Salt and pepper to taste
- 1 oz. cooked lean protein of your choice, cut into small pieces
- 2 tbsp. shredded cheese of your choice (or 1 wedge of Laughing Cow Light + 1 tbsp. shredded cheese)
- 2 tbsp. salsa

Directions:

Spray a skillet or a griddle pan with nonstick cooking spray, set it over medium heat and allow it to get hot.

Pour beaten eggs and swirl pan to full coat with eggs. Allow eggs to cook about 90 seconds.

When eggs are mostly set (there will still be liquid on top), run a wide spatula underneath the entire sheet of egg, lift it straight up, and then flip it. Cook for an additional minute.

Transfer egg sheet to a plate, laying it flat. Place vegetables and meat in the same pan. Cook until warmed through and veggies are desired consistency.

Place veggie/meat mixture to the right side of sheet of egg, aligning your fillings vertically, leaving about ½ inch overhang (the way you would a wrap or a burrito). Fold the overhang over the meat/veggie filling then continue rolling until you have an egg tube.

Top with salsa and cheese. If it's cooled down a bit from the start of cooking microwave about 30 seconds to melt cheese and reheat!

Spot Check: If this is still too much food for you, no worries! I've had Foodies use even less eggs (by separating them or using liquid egg substitute) to make them smaller!

---

* My Version has _____ calories, _____ total carbohydrates, _____ fiber, _____ sugar, _____ protein

Sunshine Breakfast Ramekin*

This is a total knock off from a "restaurant-I-can't-name-but-you-might-have-heard-of-their-sausage-made-down-on-the-farm." This is essentially a smaller version of their recipe with a reduced amount of fat. And I nixed the gravy, but you are welcome to add it back in! You'll need a four ounce ramekin for this one.

Ingredients:

- 1 tbsp. onion, diced very small
- 2 tbsp. any veggies you like, diced very small
- 1 oz. turkey or vegetarian sausage crumbles
- 1 egg, beaten (or equivalent amount of liquid egg substitute)
- 1 tbsp. shredded cheese of your choice

Directions:

Spray a small (7 and 1/8 inch) skillet with nonstick cooking spray, set it over medium heat and allow it to get hot.

Add vegetables and sauté about one minute before adding sausage crumbles. Stir to combine and warm sausage through. Transfer to a bowl.

Re-spray your skillet and add egg, allowing it to spread naturally, but don't swirl the pan.

Spot Check: I say don't swirl because you don't want a big egg sheet like with the Egg-chilada. Your egg pancake should fit nicely inside your ramekin with just a little bit of overhang.

Cook one to two minutes or until mostly set (there may be some liquid still on top) and then flip with a wide spatula. Cook another one to two minutes or until done on both sides.

Place egg in the ramekin and fill in with veggies. Top with cheese. If anything has cooled too much for your liking, microwave for 30 seconds.

Spot Check: If your egg has way too much overhang, simply trim it and add it to the filling. Then next time either separate the egg and just use the whites or use less liquid egg substitute if that's what you used.

---

* My Version has _____ calories, _____ total carbohydrates, _____ fiber, _____ sugar, _____ protein

Eggs Rosettes*

This recipe is a remake of something I saw in a magazine that involved making mini-quiches in a cupcake pan but instead of pie crust, it used filo dough. Well, I didn't want to use that either so I thought and I thought and I thought and I came up with…this!

This recipe is probably not for newer folks. Your stomach may not be quite ready for the texture of the finished product. I also would not recommend this as a make-ahead and freeze meal. But if you're having company over for brunch and want to sell them on the refined virtues of post-weight loss surgery eating, make this!

You'll need a muffin tin for this recipe. If you use a standard muffin tin, this makes six. If you use a mini-muffin tin (and smaller pieces of meat) it will make 12-15.

Ingredients:

- ¼ c. vegetables of your choice, diced small
- 4 eggs, beaten (or equivalent amount of liquid egg substitute)
- 1 tsp. baking powder
- ½ c. shredded cheese of your choice
- 12 slices of lean deli meat (bonus points for low-sodium meat!)
- Optional: fresh garlic, any herbs and spices you like, additional protein (1-2 oz.) for the egg filling.

Directions:

Preheat your oven to 350 degrees.

Spray a skillet with nonstick cooking spray, set it over medium heat and allow it to get hot.

Sauté veggies about two minutes or until softened. Transfer to a bowl and allow to cool.

In a separate bowl, beat eggs with baking powder, then add any spices you like. Add the cooled veggies to the egg mixture and stir.

Spray muffin tin with nonstick cooking spray and line six spots with two slices of deli meat (one atop the other to ensure no holes). Pour equal amounts of egg mixture into each meat cup. Top with cheese.

---

* My Version has _____ calories, _____ total carbohydrates, _____ fiber, _____ sugar, _____ protein

38

Bake at 350 degrees for about seven to 10 minutes or until eggs are completely cooked. Allow to cool before gently lifting cups out of the muffin tin to serve.

Spot Check: Make it festive! The more colors of vegetables you use, the prettier this is!

Chapter Three:
Smart Carbs

Some of you, of course, will think this is an oxymoron. Or blasphemy. Or that carbs are the devil.

If that's you, it's easy enough to skip this section! For the sake of not overcharging you for the extra pages it'd take to sell you on the fact that there are carbs – and, yes, starches – that can have nutritional benefit, I will simply welcome you to check out the less "starchy" sections of this book!

However, if you believe that whole grain starches, in moderation, have a place in a balanced eating plan, this section is for you!

But that doesn't mean there aren't rules. Many post-ops get what I call "very special blood sugar moments." Whether you have full-blown reactive hypoglycemia (a condition whereby your blood sugar drops in response to eating certain foods, most often starchy carbs) or starches just make you feel funny (drowsy, etc.) or nothing at all, you should always strive for meals that are protein heavy. Protein-heavy meals are recommended for post-op bariatric patients and can help avoid blood sugar issues.

So…how is it, then, that I propose integrating starches into a healthy, happy post-op life?

Turn the page and find out!

Protein Pancakes (and other breakfast diner favorites)

Yes, I said it. Pancakes. With protein. No, I'm not kidding you!

But before we get into that, let's talk a minute.

I know most people like to modify recipes. It's natural. You add a pinch of this, a dash of that, make the recipe your own! I do it, you do it, everybody does it. And of course you're welcome to do it with the recipes in this book (you bought the dang thing so, really, you *own* this process!).

However, if I might make a small suggestion…

If you are going to modify any of the protein/starchy recipes in this book, do yourself a favor and run the nutrition information in your favorite food diary to see how your changes shake out.

Because (and ONLY because) starches are so scary for most post-ops, I'm going to do something controversial. I'm going to break my "no stats" rule and give you the nutrition information <u>for the base recipes only</u>. (So any recipes that build upon that recipe, no stats, you can figure it out. I have faith in you!)

Getting back to why you should run stats on your changes…my recipes are balanced so that there's a good amount of protein per serving. It's really easy, with a few small changes, to make your dish carb-heavy instead of protein-heavy. So change the recipe all you want, but test out the stats before doing so to make sure it still fits into your healthy plan. K?

Let's do this!

The first thing you need is my basic recipe for high protein baking mix (NOTE: baking mix and pancake mix are essentially the same thing, just different marketing techniques). There are companies that sell high protein/ low-carb baking mix and if it's available to you locally, go for it. But if you don't want to make a special internet purchase, here's a basic recipe for a protein baking mix that you can keep in an airtight container or zip-top bag for up to a month.

There are two versions of this baking mix: one uses soy flour, the other uses almond meal. I know some people control the amount of soy in their eating plans, which is why I provided a variation. But don't feel limited by it! There are many alternatives to white flour such as garbanzo bean flour and white bean flour. Go online to check out your options then look for alternatives to white flour, which are often found in your grocery store's organic food aisle.

Nik's Protein Baking Mix (Version #1):

Yields approximately four 1/3 c. servings

- 1 c. Hodgson Mill soy flour
- 2 scoops BiPro USA unflavored whey powder[*] (See "Where to Buy" on pg. 143 for details)
- 1 tsp. baking powder
- ¼ tsp. salt

Nutrition information (entire batch): 480 calories, 0g fat, 40g carbs, 24g fiber, 16g sugar, 96g protein

Nutrition information (per 1/3 c. serving): 120 calories, 0g fat, 10g carbs, 6g fiber, 4g sugars, 24g protein

Nik's Protein Baking Mix (Version #2):

Yields approximately four 1/3 c. servings
(This is the soy-free alternative to the protein baking mix recipe)

- ½ c. almond meal
- 4 scoops BiPro USA unflavored whey powder
- 2 tsp. baking powder
- ¼ tsp. salt

Nutrition information (entire batch): 640 calories, 28g fat, 12g carbs, 6g fiber, 2g sugar, 92g protein.

Nutrition information (per 1/3 c. serving): 160 calories, 7g fat, 3g carbs, 1g fiber, <1g sugar, 23g protein.

---

[*] If you'd like to substitute another protein powder for the BiPro, use two servings of a protein powder that is about 80-100 calories and 20g of protein per serving. There should be very few grams of fat and carbohydrates (less than three grams of either) and very little, if any sugar. If you use different ingredients, use the guide to calculating nutrition information (on pg. 137) to calculate nutrition information based on what you used.

Protein Pancakes[*]

(Makes 4-6 small pancakes)

Ingredients:

- 1 serving Nik's Protein Baking Mix
- 2 tbsp. unflavored Greek yogurt (Note: Use 1 or 2% but not fat free)
- 1 egg, beaten (or equivalent amount of liquid egg substitute)
- ¼ tsp. pure vanilla extract
- 1 tsp. no-calorie sweetener, or to taste
- For topping: ¼ c. sugar-free pancake syrup or same amount of sugar-free fruit compote (recipe included)

Directions:

Spray a griddle with nonstick cooking spray, set it over medium heat and allow it to get hot.

Meanwhile, combine all ingredients in a bowl and mix thoroughly. If mixture is too thick, add milk, by the tablespoon, until it reaches the consistency of not-quite-set pudding.

Use a tablespoon to drop heaps of batter onto your skillet and spread them into rounds. Cook about one to two minutes before flipping and cooking on the other side. Transfer to plate when done.

Spot Check: Pancakes get their fluffiness from the fat in the recipe. Because these are reduced fat and higher protein, they will be heartier pancakes.

Spot Check: This base recipe can also be used to make protein waffles!

Spot Check: To freeze extra pancakes, individually wrap in plastic wrap and then store in a freezer-safe storage bag.

Nutrition Information:

For baking mix, version #1: 198 calories, 5g fat, 10g carbs, 6g fiber, 4g sugars, 31.6g protein

For baking mix, version #2: 238 calories, 12g fat, 3 g carbs, <1 g fiber, <1g sugars, 30.6g protein

---

[*] My Version has _____ calories, _____ total carbohydrates, _____ fiber, _____ sugar, _____ protein

Peanut Butter Pancakes[*]

Ingredients:

- 1 serving Nik's Protein Baking Mix
- 2 tbsp. peanut flour (see the "where to buy" section on pg. 143)
- 2 tbsp. unflavored Greek yogurt (Note: Use 1 or 2% but not fat free)
- 3 tbsp. milk (any kind of milk works here)
- 1 egg, beaten (or equivalent amount of liquid egg substitute)
- ¼ tsp. pure vanilla extract
- 1 tsp. no-calorie sweetener, or to taste

Directions:

Spray a griddle with nonstick cooking spray, set it over medium heat and allow it to get hot.

Meanwhile, combine all ingredients in a bowl and mix thoroughly. If mixture is too thick, add milk, by the tablespoon, until it reaches the consistency of not-quite-set pudding.

Use a tablespoon to drop heaps of batter onto your skillet and spread them into rounds. Cook about one to two minutes before flipping and cooking on the other side. Transfer to plate when done.

Spot Check: Pancakes get their fluffiness from the fat in the recipe. Because these are reduced fat and higher protein, they will be heartier pancakes.

Spot Check: This base recipe can also be used to make protein waffles!

Spot Check: To freeze extra pancakes, individually wrap in plastic wrap and then store in a freezer-safe storage bag.

---

[*] My Version has _____ calories, _____ total carbohydrates, _____ fiber, _____ sugar, _____ protein

Blueberry Pancakes[*]

Ingredients:

- 1 serving Nik's Protein Baking Mix + 1 additional tablespoon
- 2 tbsp. unflavored Greek yogurt (Note: Use 1 or 2% but not fat free)
- 3 tbsp. milk (any kind of milk works here)
- 1 egg, beaten (or equivalent amount of liquid egg substitute)
- ¼ tsp. pure vanilla extract
- ¼ c. fresh blueberries
- 1 tsp. no-calorie sweetener, or to taste

Directions:

Spray a griddle with nonstick cooking spray, set it over medium heat and allow it to get hot.

Meanwhile, combine all ingredients (except blueberries and one tablespoon of baking mix) in a bowl and mix thoroughly. If mixture is too thick, add milk, by the tablespoon, until it reaches the consistency of not-quite-set pudding.

In a separate bowl, shake blueberries in one tablespoon of baking mix and be sure to coat thoroughly.

Spot Check: Shaking blueberries in the baking mix will help them not sink to the bottom of the pancakes when you add them to the batter.

Use a tablespoon to drop heaps of batter onto your skillet and spread them into rounds. Quickly press blueberries into pancakes, cook one to two minutes, then flip and cook on the other side. Transfer to plate when done.

Spot Check: Pancakes get their fluffiness from the fat in the recipe. Because these are reduced fat and higher protein, they will be heartier pancakes.

Spot Check: This base recipe can also be used to make protein waffles!

Spot Check: To freeze extra pancakes, individually wrap in plastic wrap and then store in a freezer-safe storage bag.

---

[*] My Version has _____ calories, _____ total carbohydrates, _____ fiber, _____ sugar, _____ protein

Apple Cinnamon Pancakes[*]

Ingredients:

- 1 serving Nik's Protein Baking Mix
- 2 tbsp. unflavored Greek yogurt (Note: Use 1 or 2% but not fat free)
- 3 tbsp. milk (any kind of milk works here)
- 1 egg, beaten (or equivalent amount of liquid egg substitute)
- ¼ tsp. pure vanilla extract
- 2 tbsp. diced apples (skins removed)
- ¼ tsp. cinnamon OR apple pie spice
- 1 tsp. no-calorie sweetener, or to taste

Directions:

Spray a griddle with nonstick cooking spray, set it over medium heat and allow it to get hot.

Meanwhile, combine all ingredients in a bowl and mix thoroughly. If mixture is too thick, add milk, by the tablespoon, until it reaches the consistency of not-quite-set pudding.

Use a tablespoon measure to drop heaps of batter onto your skillet and spread them into rounds. Cook for one to two minutes, then flip and cook on the other side. Transfer to plate when done.

Spot Check: Pancakes get their fluffiness from the fat in the recipe. Because these are reduced fat and higher protein, they will be heartier pancakes.

Spot Check: This base recipe can also be used to make protein waffles!

Spot Check: To freeze extra pancakes, individually wrap in plastic wrap and then store in a freezer-safe storage bag.

---

* My Version has _____ calories, _____ total carbohydrates, _____ fiber, _____ sugar, _____ protein

Cinnamon Bun Pancakes[*]

Ingredients:

- 1 serving Nik's Protein Baking Mix
- 2 tbsp. unsweetened apple sauce
- 3 tbsp. milk (any kind of milk works here)
- 1 egg, beaten (or equivalent amount of liquid egg substitute)
- ¼ tsp. pure vanilla extract
- 1 tsp. no-calorie sweetener, or to taste.
- ¼ tsp. cinnamon
- 1 oz. sugar-free pancake syrup

Topping:

- 1 oz. low-fat cream cheese
- 1-2 tbsp. no-calorie sweetener of your choice

Directions:

Spray a griddle with nonstick cooking spray, set it over medium heat and allow it to get hot.

In a bowl, combine baking mix, apple sauce, milk, egg, vanilla, sweetenner, cinnamon and pancake syrup. Mix well. If batter seems too thick, add milk by the tablespoon until the consistency is like that of not-quite-set pudding.

Drop tablespoons of batter onto the griddle and shape into rounds. Cook one to two minutes, then flip and cook the other side. Transfer to a plate when done.

To make the topping: Microwave cream cheese on high heat for one minute or until very soft. Add sweetener and mix. Top pancakes with cream cheese mixture!

Spot Check: To freeze extra pancakes, individually wrap in plastic wrap and then store in a freezer-safe storage bag.

---

[*] My Version has _____ calories, _____ total carbohydrates, _____ fiber, _____ sugar, _____ protein

48

Chocolate Chip Pancakes*

Ingredients:

- 1 serving Nik's Protein Baking Mix + additional teaspoon
- 2 tbsp. unflavored Greek yogurt (Note: Use 1 or 2% but not fat free)
- 3 tbsp. milk (any kind of milk works here)
- 1 egg, beaten (or equivalent amount of liquid egg substitute)
- ¼ tsp. pure vanilla extract
- 1 serving sugar-free mini-chocolate chips (check the package for the serving size)
- 1 tsp. no-calorie sweetener, or to taste

Directions:

Spray a griddle with nonstick cooking spray, set it over medium heat and allow it to get hot.

Meanwhile, combine all ingredients (except chocolate chips and one tablespoon of baking mix) in a bowl and mix thoroughly. If mixture is too thick, add milk, by the tablespoon, until it reaches the consistency of not-quite-set pudding.

In a separate bowl, shake chocolate chips in one teaspoon of baking mix and be sure to coat thoroughly.

Spot Check: Shaking chocolate chips in the baking mix will help them not sink to the bottom of the pancakes when you add them to the batter.

Use a tablespoon to drop heaps of batter onto your skillet and spread them into rounds. Quickly drop chocolate chips into pancakes, cook for one to two minutes, then flip and cook on the other side. Transfer to plate when done.

Spot Check: Pancakes get their fluffiness from the fat in the recipe. Because these are reduced fat and higher protein, they will be heartier pancakes.

Spot Check: This base recipe can also be used to make protein waffles!

Spot Check: To freeze extra pancakes, individually wrap in plastic wrap and then store in a freezer-safe storage bag.

---

* My Version has _____ calories, _____ total carbohydrates, _____ fiber, _____ sugar, _____ protein

49

Bananas Foster Pancakes[*]

Ingredients:

- 1 serving Nik's Protein Baking Mix + additional teaspoon
- 1 tbsp. sugar-free banana pudding mix
- 2 tbsp. unflavored Greek yogurt (Note: Use 1 or 2% but not fat free)
- 3 tbsp. milk (any kind of milk works here)
- 1 egg, beaten (or equivalent amount of liquid egg substitute)
- ¼ tsp. pure vanilla extract

For topping:

- A few sprays no or low-calorie butter spray
- ¼ banana, cut into slices of desired thickness
- ¼ c. sugar-free pancake syrup
- 1/8 tsp. rum extract
- 1/8 tsp. cinnamon

Directions:

Spray a griddle with nonstick cooking spray, set it over medium heat and allow it to get hot.

Meanwhile, combine all ingredients in a bowl and mix thoroughly. If mixture is too thick, add milk, by the tablespoon, until it reaches the consistency of not-quite-set pudding.

Use a tablespoon to drop heaps of batter onto your skillet and spread them into rounds. Cook about one to two minutes before flipping and cooking on the other side. Transfer to plate when done.

To make topping: Spray down a small skillet (like 7 and 1/8 inch) with nonstick cooking spray, set it over medium heat and allow it to get hot. Add bananas and spray with butter spray. Cook about one minute before adding pancake syrup. Allow it to come to a low boil, then drop the temperature down. Add rum extract and cinnamon and stir, then top pancakes.

Spot Check: Pancakes get their fluffiness from the fat in the recipe. Because these are reduced fat and higher protein, they will be heartier pancakes.

Spot Check: This base recipe can also be used to make protein waffles!

Spot Check: To freeze extra pancakes, individually wrap in plastic wrap and then store in a freezer-safe storage bag.

---

[*] My Version has _____ calories, _____ total carbohydrates, _____ fiber, _____ sugar, _____ protein

Bacon & Salted Caramel Pancakes[*]
(Don't knock it 'til you try it!)

Ingredients:

- 1 serving Nik's Protein Baking Mix + additional teaspoon
- 1 tbsp. sugar-free banana pudding mix
- 2 tbsp. unflavored Greek yogurt (Note: Use 1 or 2% but not fat free)
- 3 tbsp. milk (any kind of milk works here)
- 1 egg, beaten (or equivalent amount of liquid egg substitute)
- ¼ tsp. pure vanilla extract
- 1 tsp. no-calorie sweetener, or to taste
- 1 heaping tbsp. bacon bits (or ½ slice of cooked bacon, crumbled)
- Topping: 1 tbsp. sugar-free caramel sauce and a pinch of kosher or finishing salt (large-crystal salt)

Directions:

Spray a griddle with nonstick cooking spray, set it over medium heat and allow it to get hot.

Meanwhile, combine all ingredients (except bacon bits) in a bowl and mix thoroughly. If mixture is too thick, add milk, by the tablespoon, until it reaches the consistency of not-quite-set pudding. Add bacon bits to the batter and mix thoroughly.

Use a tablespoon to drop heaps of batter onto your skillet and spread them into rounds. Cook about one to two minutes before flipping and cooking on the other side. Transfer to plate when done.

To make topping: Put caramel sauce in a microwave-safe cup and cook for 30 seconds on high heat. Drizzle over pancakes and then top with salt.

Spot Check: To freeze extra pancakes, individually wrap in plastic wrap and then store in a freezer-safe storage bag.

---

* My Version has _____ calories, _____ total carbohydrates, _____ fiber, _____ sugar, _____ protein

French Toast[*]

Ingredients:

- 1 slice P-28 high protein bread (see "Where to buy" on pg. 143)
- 1 egg white, beaten (or 1 tbsp. liquid egg substitute)
- 2 tbsp. milk (whatever kind you use)
- ¼ tsp. pure vanilla extract
- A dash of cinnamon
- 1 tsp. no-calorie sweetener, or to taste
- Topping ideas: ¼ c. sugar-free pancake syrup, ¼ c. sugar-free fruit compote (recipe pg. 54) or 2 tbsp. nutty syrup topping (recipe pg. 53)
- Substitution: If you can't find high protein bread, you can get very thin sliced whole wheat bread and add ½ tbsp. of vanilla flavored protein powder to your egg wash.

Directions:

Spray a griddle with nonstick cooking spray, set it over medium heat and allow it to get hot.

In a bowl combine egg white, milk, vanilla and cinnamon. Dredge bread slice in the egg mixture on both sides and lay on the griddle.

Cook two minutes one side before flipping and cooking on the other side. Transfer to plate when done and add desired toppings.

Nutrition Information: 170 calories, 4g fat, 12g carbs, 2g fiber, 3g sugars, 16g protein.

---

[*] My Version has _____ calories, _____ total carbohydrates, _____ fiber, _____ sugar, _____ protein

Nutty Syrup Topping[*]

Ingredients:

- 2 tbsp. walnut pieces
- ¼ c. sugar-free pancake syrup
- A dash of cinnamon

Directions:

Set a small skillet over medium heat (do not spray with nonstick cooking spray) and allow it to get hot. Add walnuts and cook about two minutes, or until the nuts become fragrant.

Add syrup and cinnamon, stir and warm through.

Spot Check: In addition to making a great topping for French toast, when cooled this is also a great topping for protein ice cream! There's more information about protein ice cream in The Bariatric Foodie Guide to Perfect Protein Shakes. See "Where to buy" on pg. 143 for ordering details.

---

* My Version has _____ calories, _____ total carbohydrates, _____ fiber, _____ sugar, _____ protein

Nik's "Quickie" Compotes[*]

These fruity toppings can be used on protein pancakes, protein French toast, in Greek yogurt or on cottage cheese even! These recipes are make enough for one to two servings (depending on your eating capacity), so you aren't stuck wondering what to do with them afterward.

Basic Apple

Ingredients:

- 1 small apple, peeled, cored and sliced (I recommend Pink Lady, although you can use what YOU like)
- ¼ tsp. corn starch
- 1 packet of True Lemon or ¼ tsp. lemon juice
- 2 tbsp. water
- A generous pinch of apple pie spice
- 1-2 tbsp. (depending on your taste) no calorie sweetener

Basic Blueberry

Ingredients:

- ¼ c. fresh blueberries, washed
- ¼ tsp. corn starch
- 1 packet of True Lemon or ¼ tsp. lemon juice
- 1-2 tbsp. (depending on your taste) no calorie sweetener
- 2 tbsp. water

Basic Strawberry

Ingredients:

- ¼ c. frozen chopped strawberries (or equivalent amount hulled and sliced)
- ¼ tsp. corn starch
- 1 packet of True Lemon or ¼ tsp. lemon juice
- 1-2 tbsp. (depending on your taste) no calorie sweetener
- 2 tbsp. water

---

* My Version has _____ calories, _____ total carbohydrates, _____ fiber, _____ sugar, _____ protein

Directions:

In a microwave-safe bowl, toss fruit with corn starch until well coated. Add water and sweetener and microwave on high for 1 minute. Stir and, if still not soft enough for your liking, microwave in 15 second increments until it reaches desired texture. Serve warm!

Protein Mini-Muffins[*]

These tasty little muffins are a perfect bite to start your morning. If you are a donut or pastry type of person, this section is for you! There are lots of ideas starting on the next page, but here's the base recipe. That way you can play with it and come up with your own yummy variations!

To make these mini-muffins you'll need:

- A 24-slot mini-muffin pan (nonstick is preferable)
- If you have a mini-muffin pan that isn't nonstick, mini-cupcake liners
- Nonstick cooking spray for baking (available at most grocery stores)

Ingredients:

- 2 servings Nik's protein baking mix
- ½ tsp. baking powder (yes, this is in addition to what's already in the baking mix)
- 1 large egg, beaten (or equivalent amount of liquid egg substitute)
- ¼ c. milk
- ¼ c. unsweetened applesauce
- 1 tsp. pure vanilla extract
- ¼ c. no-calorie sweetener, to taste

Directions:

Mix together all ingredients in a bowl with any additions you like (see the following pages for a few ideas). Use a half-tablespoon measuring spoon to fill a 24-slot mini-muffin tin. Each slot should be filled at least ¾ of the way.

Bake at 350 for about 15 minutes or until a toothpick inserted comes out clean. Cool entire pan on a cooling rack for 10 minutes, then remove muffins.

Store in an airtight, zip-top bag or freeze in a freezer storage bag.

Spot Check: These muffins keep in the refrigerator about a week and for two months in the freezer.

Nutrition information (entire batch):
For baking Mix, version #1: 410 calories, 0g fat, 28g carbs, 14g fiber, 10g sugars, 55g protein
For baking Mix, version #2: 490 calories, 14g fat, 18g carbs, 2g fiber, 1g sugar, 51g protein

NOTE: Divide total batch nutrition by the number of muffins the recipe yielded for you!

---

[*] My Version has _____ calories, _____ total carbohydrates, _____ fiber, _____ sugar, _____ protein

Blueberry Muffins[*]

Ingredients:

- 2 servings Nik's protein baking mix + 1 additional (separate) tablespoon
- ½ tsp. baking powder (yes, this is in addition to what's already in the baking mix)
- 1 large egg, beaten (or equivalent amount of liquid egg substitute)
- ¼ c. milk
- ¼ c. unsweetened applesauce
- 1 tsp. pure vanilla extract
- ¼ c. no-calorie sweetener, to taste
- ½ c. fresh blueberries

Directions:

In a medium mixing bowl, combine two servings of baking mix, baking powder, egg, milk, apple sauce, vanilla extract and sweetener. Combine thoroughly.

In a separate bowl, shake blueberries and one tablespoon of baking mix until berries are well coated. Discard additional baking mix, then pour berries into batter and mix.

Spot Check: Coating the berries with the baking mix helps them not sink to the bottom of the muffins.

Use a half-tablespoon measuring spoon to fill a 24-slot mini-muffin tin. Each slot should be filled at least ¾ of the way.

Bake at 350 for about 15 minutes or until a toothpick inserted comes out clean. Cool entire pan on a cooling rack for 10 minutes, then remove muffins.

Store in an airtight, zip-top bag or freeze in a freezer storage bag.

Spot Check: These muffins keep in the refrigerator about a week and for two months in the freezer.

---

* My Version has _____ calories, _____ total carbohydrates, _____ fiber, _____ sugar, _____ protein

Carrot Muffins[*]

Ingredients:

- 2 servings Nik's protein baking mix
- ½ tsp. baking powder (yes, this is in addition to what's already in the baking mix)
- 1 large egg, beaten (or equivalent amount of liquid egg substitute)
- ¼ c. milk
- ¼ c. unsweetened applesauce
- ¼ c. no-calorie sweetener, to taste
- 1 tsp. pure vanilla extract
- 1/3 c. grated carrots
- ¼ tsp. cinnamon
- 1/8 tsp. nutmeg
- 1/8 tsp. ground ginger
- Optional: 2-3 tbsp. raisins, rinsed of sugar coating

Directions:

In a medium mixing bowl, combine baking mix, baking powder, egg, milk, apple sauce and sweetener. Combine thoroughly.

Add vanilla, carrots and spices and mix again. If using, add raisins last and mix one more time.

Use a half-tablespoon measuring spoon to fill a 24-slot mini-muffin tin. Each slot should be filled at least ¾ of the way.

Bake at 350 for about 15 minutes or until a toothpick inserted comes out clean. Cool entire pan on a cooling rack for 10 minutes, then remove muffins.

Store in an airtight, zip-top bag or freeze in a freezer storage bag.

Spot Check: These muffins keep in the refrigerator about a week and for two months in the freezer.

---

* My Version has _____ calories, _____ total carbohydrates, _____ fiber, _____ sugar, _____ protein

Pumpkin Muffins[*]

Ingredients:

- 2 servings Nik's protein baking mix
- ½ tsp. baking powder (yes, this is in addition to what's already in the baking mix)
- 1 large egg, beaten (or equivalent amount of liquid egg substitute)
- ¼ c. milk
- ¼ c. pumpkin puree (not pumpkin pie filling!)
- ¼ c. no-calorie sweetener, to taste
- 1 tsp. pure vanilla extract
- ¼ tsp. pumpkin pie spice

Directions:

In a medium mixing bowl, combine all ingredients and mix well.

Use a half-tablespoon measuring spoon to fill a 24-slot mini-muffin tin. Each slot should be filled at least ¾ of the way.

Bake at 350 for about 15 minutes or until a toothpick inserted comes out clean. Cool entire pan on a cooling rack for 10 minutes, then remove muffins.

Store in an airtight, zip-top bag or freeze in a freezer storage bag.

Spot Check: These muffins keep in the refrigerator about a week and for two months in the freezer.

---

* My Version has _____ calories, _____ total carbohydrates, _____ fiber, _____ sugar, _____ protein

Chocolate Muffins[*]

Ingredients:

- 2 servings Nik's protein baking mix
- ½ tsp. baking powder (yes, this is in addition to what's already in the baking mix)
- 1 large egg, beaten (or equivalent amount of liquid egg substitute)
- ¼ c. milk
- ¼ c. unsweetened applesauce
- 3 tbsp. unsweetened cocoa powder
- 1 tsp. good instant decaffeinated coffee crystals
- 1 tsp. pure vanilla extract
- ¼ c. no-calorie sweetener, to taste

Directions:

In a medium mixing bowl, combine all ingredients and mix well.

Use a half-tablespoon measuring spoon to fill a 24-slot mini-muffin tin. Each slot should be filled at least ¾ of the way.

Bake at 350 for about 15 minutes or until a toothpick inserted comes out clean. Cool entire pan on a cooling rack for 10 minutes, then remove muffins.

Store in an airtight, zip-top bag or freeze in a freezer storage bag.

Spot Check: These muffins keep in the refrigerator about a week and for two months in the freezer.

---

* My Version has _____ calories, _____ total carbohydrates, _____ fiber, _____ sugar, _____ protein

Apple Cinnamon Muffins[*]

Ingredients:

- 2 servings Nik's protein baking mix
- ½ tsp. baking powder (yes, this is in addition to what's already in the baking mix)
- 1 large egg, beaten (or equivalent amount of liquid egg substitute)
- ¼ c. milk
- ¼ c. unsweetened applesauce
- 1 tsp. pure vanilla extract
- ¼ c. no-calorie sweetener, to taste
- 1 small apple, peeled, cored, seeded and diced
- ½ tbsp. cinnamon
- Optional: ¼ c. raisins, rinsed of any sugar coating

Directions:

In a medium mixing bowl, combine baking mix, baking powder, egg, milk, apple sauce and sweetener. Combine thoroughly.

Add vanilla, apples and cinnamon and mix again. If using, add raisins last and mix one more time.

Use a half-tablespoon measuring spoon to fill a 24-slot mini-muffin tin. Each slot should be filled at least ¾ of the way.

Bake at 350 for about 15 minutes or until a toothpick inserted comes out clean. Cool entire pan on a cooling rack for 10 minutes, then remove muffins.

Store in an airtight, zip-top bag or freeze in a freezer storage bag.

Spot Check: These muffins keep in the refrigerator about a week and for two months in the freezer.

---

* My Version has _____ calories, _____ total carbohydrates, _____ fiber, _____ sugar, _____ protein

Breakfast Pizzas

No, really!

I know, you thought things like pizza were off limits but I'm going to clue you in on how you can have a breakfast pizza (and, really, this applies to the concept of pizza as a whole) without wrecking your plan. You ready?

First, let's talk crust. Most pizzas have a flour crust – a white flour crust, to be specific. That's no good for us. What I use instead is a whole-wheat, low-carb tortilla or flatbread. There are several kinds that work well, including:

- La Banderita low-carb, whole wheat tortillas (I suggest taco size for us)
- La Tortilla Factory low-carb, whole wheat tortillas (also taco size)
- FlatOut Light whole wheat flatbreads (they also come in "kid-sized")

Each of these options is less than 100 calories, contains a LOT of fiber and the FlatOut even contains a good bit of protein! That's the kind of crust you want for a breakfast pizza! The directions for each recipe say it, but it bears saying here that you should probably pre-bake your tortilla for five to seven minutes before adding toppings to ensure you get a nice, crisp result.

Now, let's talk toppings. The pizzas in this section are all meant to be breakfast pizzas, so they have breakfast-themed toppings. But don't let that limit you. Get creative! But do make sure you put some lean protein on that pizza and make sure all your toppings are reasonable with fat and don't contribute a lot of added sugar.

Finally, let's talk specifically about cheese. Here we come back to our different food outlooks. If you are a Food-phobe, full-fat cheese may bug you. There are plenty of reduced fat options, including fat-free cheese. I personally wouldn't recommend it but a Frankenfooder probably would, while food purists would probably only do the full-fat stuff.

I like to think of myself as a Zen goddess/Sensible eater (or the child of the two!). What does that mean? I look at what I have going on that day. If I know I'm likely to have a higher calorie day, I eat a lower calorie breakfast. If I know I can offset higher calorie items later with exercise or lighter meals, maybe I take the splurge.

The choice is yours. What I'm trying to say is that for every meal, you need to decide for yourself your own nutritional comfort level. Heck, maybe you are even skipping this section because it doesn't fit into your plan and that is absolutely fine!

For the rest of you, let's journey on!

Basic Egg & Bacon Breakfast Pizza[*]

Ingredients:

- 1 small whole-wheat, low-carb tortilla or flatbread
- 1 wedge Laughing Cow Light cheese, in any flavor you like
- 1 egg, beaten (or equivalent amount of liquid egg substitute)
- 1 heaping tbsp. bacon bits (or one slice of bacon, crumbled)
- 1 tbsp. shredded cheese, any kind you like
- Salt and pepper to taste

Directions:

Preheat your oven to 350 degrees.

Spray a cookie sheet with nonstick cooking spray and place tortilla or flatbread "crust" on it. Bake for five to seven minutes or until it just begins to get crisp.

Meanwhile, scramble your egg.

When the crust is done pre-baking, use a butter knife to spread the Laughing Cow cheese onto it. Top with eggs, then bacon, then shredded cheese.

Bake for 10 minutes or until edges brown and cheese is melted.

---

[*] My Version has _____ calories, _____ total carbohydrates, _____ fiber, _____ sugar, _____ protein

Turkey, Egg & Cheese Breakfast Pizza[*]

Ingredients:

- 1 small whole-wheat, low-carb tortilla or flatbread
- 1 tbsp. onions, diced
- 2 slices of deli-cut, low-sodium turkey, chopped up
- 1 egg, beaten (or equivalent amount of liquid egg substitute)
- 1 wedge Laughing Cow Light cheese, in any flavor you like
- 1 tbsp. shredded cheese, any kind you like
- Salt and pepper to taste

Directions:

Preheat your oven to 350 degrees.

Spray a cookie sheet with nonstick cooking spray and place tortilla or flatbread "crust" on it. Bake for five to seven minutes or until it just begins to get crisp.

Meanwhile, spray a skillet with nonstick cooking spray, set it over medium heat and allow it to get hot. Add onions and sauté one minute. Then add turkey and cook until slightly browned. Transfer to a bowl.

In the same skillet, scramble your egg.

When the crust is done pre-baking, use a butter knife to spread the Laughing Cow cheese onto it. Top with eggs, then turkey mixture, then shredded cheese.

Bake for 10 minutes or until edges brown and cheese is melted.

---

* My Version has _____ calories, _____ total carbohydrates, _____ fiber, _____ sugar, _____ protein

Mexican Breakfast Pizza[*]

Ingredients:

- 1 small whole-wheat, low-carb tortilla or flatbread
- 1 tbsp. onions, diced
- 1 tbsp. green peppers, diced
- 1 oz. chorizo sausage, casing removed
- 1 egg, beaten (or equivalent amount of liquid egg substitute)
- 1 wedge Laughing Cow Light Queso Fresco flavored cheese (although any kind you like will do!)
- 1 tbsp. Mexican blend shredded cheese (although any kind you like will do!)
- Salt and pepper to taste
- Optional toppings: 2 tbsp. unflavored Greek yogurt, salsa

Directions:

Preheat your oven to 350 degrees.

Spray a cookie sheet with nonstick cooking spray and place tortilla or flatbread "crust" on it. Bake for five to seven minutes or until it just begins to get crisp.

Meanwhile, spray a skillet with nonstick cooking spray, set it over medium heat and allow it to get hot. Add green peppers and onions and sauté one minute. Add chorizo and break meat apart (as if browning ground meat) and mix with onions and peppers. Cook until meat is done then set aside in a bowl.

In the same skillet, scramble your egg.

When the crust is done pre-baking, use a butter knife to spread the Laughing Cow cheese onto it. Top with eggs, then sausage mixture, then shredded cheese.

Bake for 10 minutes or until edges brown and cheese is melted. Top if desired.

---

[*] My Version has _____ calories, _____ total carbohydrates, _____ fiber, _____ sugar, _____ protein

Reader Submission: Linda's Turkey Quesadilla[*]

Ingredients:

- 1 high-fiber, low-carb wrap
- 2 oz. turkey lunch meat (NOTE: Use low-sodium if you have blood pressure issues)
- 2-3 strips roasted red pepper (or any cooked vegetables you like)
- 1 slice of low fat American cheese
- 2 tsp. honey mustard

Directions:

Spray skillet with non-stick cooking spray, set it over medium heat and allow it to get hot.

Place wrap on skillet for a few minutes or until it starts to brown.

Spread mustard across wrap, then place shredded turkey, chopped veggies, cheese on half of wrap.

Fold the bare side of the wrap over onto the side with the turkey and vegetables and allow it to cook about a minute longer.

Flip and cook an additional minute on the other side.

Transfer to a plate and cut into desired number of pieces.

Spot Check: High-fiber, low-carb wraps tend to have about 100 calories, about 9-11g fiber and about 6-7g protein per wrap. If you don't want leftovers, try cutting the wrap in half to make a smaller quesadilla!

---

[*] My Version has _____ calories, _____ total carbohydrates, _____ fiber, _____ sugar, _____ protein

Fresh & Fruity (Almost No-Bake) Breakfast Pizza[*]

Ingredients:

- 1 small whole-wheat, low-carb tortilla or flatbread
- A few sprays of low or no-calorie butter spray
- 1 tsp. no-calorie sweetener
- A generous pinch of cinnamon
- 1 tbsp. low-fat cream cheese (If you want to go luxurious try goat cheese or mascarpone!)
- ¼ c. Greek yogurt
- 1 heaping tablespoon unflavored or vanilla protein powder
- ½ c. sliced fresh fruit of your choosing.

Directions:

Preheat your oven to 350 degrees.

Spray a cookie sheet with nonstick cooking spray and place tortilla or flatbread "crust" on it. Spray with butter spray, then sprinkle with sweetener and cinnamon. Bake for five to seven minutes or until it just begins to get crisp.

Spot Check: If you can't eat much, slice the tortilla into halves or even fourths. Use the same amount of cream cheese/Greek yogurt topping and less fruit. If you have leftover topping, put it in a container to use for another day! It keeps up to four days in the refrigerator. I would be remiss not to point out that this particular breakfast is deliciously share-able!

Meanwhile, in a small microwave-safe bowl, heat cream cheese on high for 30 seconds. Mix with Greek yogurt and protein powder until thoroughly combined.

Once crust is done pre-baking, spread cream cheese mixture on it and top with fresh fruit.

Spot Check: Get festive! Mix different colored fruit, like kiwi and strawberries, or do seasonal fruits.

---

[*] My Version has _____ calories, _____ total carbohydrates, _____ fiber, _____ sugar, _____ protein

Churro Breakfast Flat*

Ingredients:

- 1 small whole-wheat, low-carb tortilla or flatbread
- A few sprays of low or no-calorie butter spray
- 1 tsp. no-calorie sweetener
- A generous pinch of cinnamon
- 1 tbsp. cream cheese (If you want to go luxurious try goat cheese or mascarpone!)
- ¼ c. Greek yogurt
- 1 heaping tablespoon unflavored or vanilla protein powder
- Topping: Additional sweetener/cinnamon mix, if desired.

Directions:

Preheat your oven to 350 degrees.

Spray a cookie sheet with nonstick cooking spray and place tortilla or flatbread "crust" on it. Spray with butter spray, then sprinkle with sweetener and cinnamon. Bake for seven to 10 minutes or until very crisp and browned around the edges.

Meanwhile, in a small microwave-safe bowl, heat cream cheese on high for 30 seconds. Mix with Greek yogurt and protein powder until thoroughly combined.

Once crust is done pre-baking, spread cream cheese mixture on it and top if desired.

---

* My Version has _____ calories, _____ total carbohydrates, _____ fiber, _____ sugar, _____ protein

Protein Oatmeal

Oatmeal is one of those foods that seem to perplex weight loss surgery post-ops. Before surgery, it was a healthy choice, a *heart* healthy choice – a good food to eat!

Now? You're not so sure. On the one hand, oatmeal itself hasn't changed, but your priorities have. You've been told, "Protein is the king of all ingredients, let nothing come before it!" So with that in mind, does oatmeal have a place in a healthy post-op eating plan?

I can't make that decision for you. I can only tell you what I did and do. And I eat oatmeal! It's hearty and filling (especially in the winter) and can be made many ways deliciously!

But.

Like many post-ops I'm prone to "very special blood sugar moments" if my meals are too carbohydrate heavy and unfortunately my body does not differentiate much between a Snicker bar and a bowl of oatmeal in this regard. So, I have to weight it down with some protein.

This section will teach you to do the same. A few notes:

- The first recipe, for basic protein oatmeal, will probably make several servings for many of you but it reheats wonderfully. Add a splash of milk or water when reheating and it should be just fine!
- Subsequent recipes are smaller (but may still be a bit much for some of you, so see the above point!) and call for quick oats. If you like steel cut oats or old fashioned oats, you can use either. I noted on each recipe how to change the way you add protein for those.
- As a general rule, for every ¼ c. of oatmeal you use, you would use ¼ scoop (or 1 tbsp., whichever is more) of protein.
- Lastly, if you are a person who values convenience, and like instant oatmeal packets, any of these recipes works with just one packet.

You'll also find recipes for things made *with* oatmeal, like protein baked oatmeal and the breakfast cookie recipe. All these are wonderful ways to combine oatmeal and protein to feel like you're indulging when in reality you've got a pretty well-balanced breakfast.

Enjoy!

Basic Protein Oatmeal*

Ingredients:

- ¼ c. quick oats (or the same amount of regular oats)
- ½ scoop, OR 2 tbsp., protein powder**
- ½ c. milk
- ½ c. hot water
- 1 tsp. no-calorie sweetener, or to taste

Directions:

In a bowl, completely combine oats, protein powder and sweetener.

Add milk and stir until all protein powder has soaked up the milk (mixture will be thick and pasty).

Add water and stir.

Microwave on high heat for one minute. If oats have not reached desired texture, microwave in 15 second increments, stirring in between, until desired texture is achieved, adding more water, by the tablespoon, as necessary.

Nutrition Information: 155 calories, 1.5g fat, 19.5g carbs, 2g fiber, 7g sugars, 16.5g protein

---

* My Version has _____ calories, _____ total carbohydrates, _____ fiber, _____ sugar, _____ protein
** Nutrition Information based on use of BiPro USA unflavored whey protein. Use the instructions on pg. 137 to calculate nutrition based on the ingredients you used.

Maple & Brown Sugar Protein Oatmeal[*]

Ingredients:

- 1 pouch sugar-free or no-sugar added maple and brown sugar oatmeal
- ½ scoop OR 2 tbsp. protein powder (unflavored or vanilla)
- ½ c. milk
- ½ c. hot water

Directions:

In a bowl, completely combine oats and protein powder.

Add milk and stir until all protein powder has soaked up the milk (mixture will be thick and pasty).

Add water and stir.

Microwave on high heat for one minute. If oats have not reached desired texture, microwave in 15 second increments, stirring in between, until desired texture is achieved, adding more water, by the tablespoon, as necessary.

---

* My Version has _____ calories, _____ total carbohydrates, _____ fiber, _____ sugar, _____ protein

Apples & Cinnamon Protein Oatmeal[*]

Ingredients:

- ¼ c. quick oats (or the same amount of regular oats)
- ½ scoop OR 2 tbsp. protein powder (unflavored or vanilla)
- 1 tsp. no-calorie sweetener, or to taste
- ½ c. milk
- ½ c. hot water
- ¼ apple (whatever kind you like) diced small (and peeled if you don't want to eat the skin)
- 1/8 tsp. cinnamon

Directions:

In a bowl, completely combine oats, protein powder and sweetener.

Add milk and stir until all protein powder has soaked up the milk (mixture will be thick and pasty).

Add water and stir.

Microwave on high heat for one minute. If oats have not reached desired texture, microwave in 15 second increments, stirring in between, until desired texture is achieved, adding more water, by the tablespoon, as necessary.

Once finished, add apples and cinnamon and stir to combine.

Spot Check: If you'd like, you can simply use instant oatmeal in this recipe. The rest of the ingredients and directions remain the same. If you use regular/ steel-cut oats, you'll need to cook the oats in the appropriate amount of water or milk for the amount you are making. In a separate bowl, combine equal amount protein powder and room temperature liquid until a paste forms. Add that paste directly to your hot finished oatmeal, then proceed with adding the apples and cinnamon.

---

[*] My Version has _____ calories, _____ total carbohydrates, _____ fiber, _____ sugar, _____ protein

Cinnamon Bun Protein Oatmeal[*]

Ingredients:

- ¼ c. quick oats (or the same amount of regular oats)
- ½ scoop OR 2 tbsp. protein powder (unflavored or vanilla)
- 1 tsp. no-calorie sweetener, or to taste
- ½ c. milk
- ½ c. hot water
- ¼ tsp. cinnamon
- 1 tbsp. low-fat cream cheese
- Optional: Chopped walnuts

Directions:

In a bowl, completely combine oats, protein powder and sweetener.

Add milk and stir until all protein powder has soaked up the milk (mixture will be thick and pasty).

Add water and stir.

Microwave on high heat for one minute. If oats have not reached desired texture, microwave in 15 second increments, stirring in between, until desired texture is achieved, adding more water, by the tablespoon, as necessary.

Once finished, add cinnamon and cream cheese and stir to combine.

Spot Check: If you'd like, you can simply use instant oatmeal in this recipe. The rest of the ingredients and directions remain the same. If you use regular/steel-cut oats, you'll need to cook the oats in the appropriate amount of water or milk for the amount you are making. In a separate bowl, combine equal amount protein powder and room temperature liquid until a paste forms. Add that paste directly to your hot finished oatmeal, then proceed with adding the cream cheese, cinnamon and walnuts, if using.

---

[*] My Version has _____ calories, _____ total carbohydrates, _____ fiber, _____ sugar, _____ protein

74

Peaches & Cream Protein Oatmeal[*]

Ingredients:

- ¼ c. quick oats (or the same amount of regular oats)
- ½ scoop OR 2 tbsp. protein powder (unflavored or vanilla)
- 1 tsp. no-calorie sweetener, or to taste
- ½ c. fat-free half & half
- ½ c. hot water
- 1 diced peach cup in water, drained

Directions:

In a bowl, completely combine oats, protein powder and sweetener.

Add milk and stir until all protein powder has soaked up the milk (mixture will be thick and pasty).

Add water and stir.

Microwave on high heat for one minute. If oats have not reached desired texture, microwave in 15 second increments, stirring in between, until desired texture is achieved, adding more water, by the tablespoon, as necessary.

Once finished, add peaches and stir to combine.

Spot Check: If you'd like, you can simply use instant oatmeal in this recipe (omit peaches if you do). The rest of the ingredients and directions remain the same. If you use regular/steel-cut oats, you'll need to cook the oats in the appropriate amount of water or milk for the amount you are making. In a separate bowl, combine equal amount protein powder and room temperature liquid until a paste forms. Add that paste directly to your hot finished oatmeal.

---

[*] My Version has _____ calories, _____ total carbohydrates, _____ sugar, _____ protein

Super-Chunk Protein Oatmeal[*]

Ingredients:

- ¼c. quick oats (or the same amount of regular oats)
- ½ scoop Or 2 tbsp. protein powder (unflavored or vanilla)
- 1 tsp. no-calorie sweetener, or to taste
- ½ c. milk
- ½ c. hot water
- ¼ c. chopped walnuts
- ¼ apple (whatever kind you like) diced small (and peeled if you don't want to eat the apple skin)
- ¼ c. blueberries or sliced strawberries

Directions:

In a bowl, completely combine oats, protein powder and sweetener.

Add milk and stir until all protein powder has soaked up the milk (mixture will be thick and pasty).

Add water and stir.

Microwave on high heat for one minute. If oats have not reached desired texture, microwave in 15 second increments, stirring in between, until desired texture is achieved, adding more water, by the tablespoon, as necessary.

Once finished, add nuts, apples and berries and stir to combine.

Spot Check: If you'd like, you can simply use instant oatmeal in this recipe. The rest of the ingredients and directions remain the same. If you use regular/steel-cut oats, you'll need to cook the oats in the appropriate amount of water or milk for the amount you are making. In a separate bowl, combine equal amount protein powder and room temperature liquid until a paste forms. Add that paste directly to your hot finished oatmeal, then proceed with adding the nuts, apples and berries.

---

[*] My Version has _____ calories, _____ total carbohydrates, _____ fiber, _____ sugar, _____ protein

Chocolate Chip Protein Oatmeal[*]

Ingredients:

- ¼ c. quick oats (or the same amount of regular oats)
- ½ scoop – or 2 tbsp. - protein powder (unflavored or vanilla)
- 1 tsp. no-calorie sweetener, or to taste
- ½ c. milk
- ½ c. hot water
- ½ tbsp. sugar-free chocolate chips

Directions:

In a bowl, completely combine oats, protein powder and sweetener.

Add milk and stir until all protein powder has soaked up the milk (mixture will be thick and pasty).

Add water and stir.

Microwave on high heat for one minute. If oats have not reached desired texture, microwave in 15 second increments, stirring in between, until desired texture is achieved, adding more water, by the tablespoon, as necessary.

Once finished, add chocolate chips and stir to combine.

Spot Check: If you'd like, you can simply use instant oatmeal in this recipe. The rest of the Ingredients: and directions remain the same. If you use regular/ steel-cut oats, you'll need to cook the oats in the appropriate amount of water or milk for the amount you are making. In a separate bowl, combine equal amount protein powder and room temperature liquid until a paste forms. Add that paste directly to your hot finished oatmeal, then proceed with adding the chocolate chips.

------

[*] My Version has _____ calories, _____ total carbohydrates, _____ fiber, _____ sugar, _____ protein

Peanut Butter Chocolate Chip Protein Oatmeal[*]

Ingredients:

- ¼ c. quick oats (or the same amount of regular oats)
- ½ scoop OR 2 tbsp. protein powder (unflavored or vanilla)
- 1 tsp. no-calorie sweetener, or to taste
- ½ c. milk
- ½ c. hot water
- 2 tbsp. peanut flour (brand names PB2 or Chike PB – see "Where to Buy" on pg. 143)
- ½ tbsp. sugar-free chocolate chips

Directions:

In a bowl, completely combine oats, protein powder and sweetener.

Add milk and stir until all protein powder has soaked up the milk (mixture will be thick and pasty).

Add water and stir.

Microwave on high heat for one minute. If oats have not reached desired texture, microwave in 15 second increments, stirring in between, until desired texture is achieved, adding more water, by the tablespoon, as necessary.

Once finished, add peanut flour and stir. Finally, add chocolate chips and stir again to combine.

Spot Check: If you'd like, you can simply use instant oatmeal in this recipe. The rest of the Ingredients: and directions remain the same. If you use regular/ steel-cut oats, you'll need to cook the oats in the appropriate amount of water or milk for the amount you are making. In a separate bowl, combine equal amount protein powder and room temperature liquid until a paste forms. Add that paste directly to your hot finished oatmeal, then proceed with adding the peanut flour and chocolate chips.

---

* My Version has _____ calories, _____ total carbohydrates, _____ fiber, _____ sugar, _____ protein

Baked Protein Oatmeal

What the heck is baked protein oatmeal?

(Don't lie, you said that, in your head, when you read this – I heard you!)

I first experienced baked oatmeal in a place where I experience a lot of great food. At the Amish market. Here in my neck of the woods, there is a wonderful Amish market where they sell everything from nuts, fruits, vegetables and fresh meat to things like those cookies you use to make ice cream sandwiches, the cheesy powder that goes on cheese popcorn (no, I'm not kidding) and crystalized fructose!

The Amish also have a café where, for a mere $5 they will serve you a hunk of baked oatmeal, which is made, obviously, out of oatmeal but has other things in it. Texture-wise, it's half way between a cake and a cereal bar and it is GOOD!

The problem is, in its regular form, it is sugary! So after I had surgery, I set out to make this wonderful breakfast work for my new lifestyle.

The recipes that follow make 8 inch by 8 inch pans of baked protein oatmeal. A few rules of thumb here:

- Yes, this does freeze well. I recommend cutting it into squares, wrapping each square in plastic wrap, then putting all the squares in a freezer storage bag.
- The length of time you bake determines the texture. In the recipes I put a time range. The low end of the range will yield a soft, cakey breakfast treat. The higher end of the range will be more like a breakfast bar.
- If you ever over-cook your baked oatmeal, no worries! When eating, just wrap a slice in a wet paper towel and nuke it about 15 to 20 seconds. It'll soften nicely!

I've given you some starter ideas in this section but I invite you to be inspired! Since I first started posting about baked protein oatmeal on the Bariatric Foodie site, folks have sent me their own unique creations. If you come up with a version you love, be sure to send a picture and recipe to bariatricfoodie@yahoo.com. I'd love to feature it on the site!

Basic Baked Protein Oatmeal[*]

(This is a base recipe upon which you can customize as you like. On the pages that follow there are different flavors to give you some ideas)

Dry Ingredients:

- 1 c. quick oats
- 2 scoops vanilla protein powder[**]
- 1/8 tsp. salt (a generous pinch)

Wet Ingredients:

- 1 + ¼ c. milk
- ¼ c. no-calorie sweetener, to taste
- 1 tsp. cinnamon
- 1 tsp. vanilla extract (or for this I used hazelnut extract)
- 1 egg, beaten (or equivalent amount of liquid egg substitute)

Directions:

Preheat your oven to 350 degrees.

In a bowl whisk together dry ingredients until well mixed.

In another bowl, combine milk and [K6]no-calorie sweetener and whisk before adding beaten egg and whisking again.

Add wet ingredients to dry and stir until everything is mixed.

Spray an 8 inch x 8 inch baking dish with nonstick cooking spray and pour mixture into it.

For a softer baked oatmeal: Bake at 350 for 12-15 minutes or until top is just set. Remove from oven (and turn oven off) but cool on top of oven.

For firmer oatmeal squares: Bake at 350 for 15-20 minutes or until top is set and edges are browned. Cool on cooling rack away from oven.

Spot Check: When using steel-cut or old-fashioned oats, increase milk by ½ cup, drop the temperature to 325 degrees. Cook time varies between 35 – 55 minutes, depending on your oven. Oats are done when solid, browned and spoon leaves an indentation.

Nutrition information: 770 calories, 17g fat, 84g carbs, 8g fiber, 76g protein (for entire batch - divide by your number of servings!)

---

[*]   My Version has _____ calories, _____ total carbohydrates, _____ fiber, _____ sugar, _____ protein

[**] I used Pure Protein Vanilla flavored protein powder for this recipe. If you use a different protein powder, your nutrition information may vary. Be sure to use the instructions on pg. 137 to figure out the nutrition information for the ingredients you used.

Fall Harvest Baked Protein Oatmeal[*]

Dry Ingredients:

- 1 c. quick oats
- 2 scoops vanilla protein powder
- 1/8 tsp. salt (a generous pinch)
- 1 tsp. pumpkin pie spice
- ½ c. whatever chopped nuts you like (I used pecans but walnuts might be nice too)

Wet Ingredients:

- 1 + ¼ c. milk
- ½ c. pumpkin puree (not pumpkin pie filling)
- ¼ c. sugar-free maple flavored pancake syrup
- ¼ c. no-calorie sweetener
- 1 tsp. vanilla extract (or for this I used hazelnut extract)
- 1 egg, beaten (or equivalent amount of liquid egg substitute)

Directions:

Preheat your oven to 350 degrees.

In a bowl whisk together dry ingredients until well mixed.

In another bowl, combine milk, pumpkin, syrup and no-calorie sweetener and whisk before adding beaten egg and whisking again.

Add wet ingredients to dry and stir until everything is mixed.

Spray an 8 inch x 8 inch baking dish with nonstick cooking spray and pour mixture into it.

For a softer baked oatmeal: Bake at 350 for 12-15 minutes or until top is just set. Remove from oven (and turn oven off) but cool on top of oven.

For firmer oatmeal squares: Bake at 350 for 15-20 minutes or until top is set and edges are browned. Cool on cooling rack away from oven.

Spot Check: When using steel-cut or old-fashioned oats, increase milk by ½ cup, drop the temperature to 325 degrees. Cook time varies between 35 – 55 minutes, depending on your oven. Oats are done when solid, browned and spoon leaves an indentation.

---

[*] My Version has _____ calories, _____ total carbohydrates, _____ fiber, _____ sugar, _____ protein

Nutty Apple Baked Protein Oatmeal[*]

Dry Ingredients:

- 1 c. quick oats
- 1/3 c. vanilla or unflavored protein powder
- A generous pinch of salt
- ½ tsp. cinnamon

Wet Ingredients:

- 1.5 c. milk
- ¼ c. sugar-free pancake syrup
- 2 eggs, beaten OR ½ c. liquid egg substitute[K12]
- ¼ c. PB2 powdered peanut butter
- Optional: ¼ c. natural peanut butter (It bumps up the peanut flavor), additional sweetener, to taste

Chunky Stuff:

- 1 medium-sized apple, cut into small cubes[K13] (Note: peel if you do not want to eat the apple skin)
- ¼ c. chopped walnuts

Directions:

Preheat your oven to 350 degrees.

Mix all dry ingredients together in a mixing bowl. Set aside.

Mix together all wet ingredients in another bowl. Add to dry ingredients and combine thoroughly.

Add chunky stuff and mix thoroughly. Pour into an 8 inch x 8 inch baking dish that has been sprayed in nonstick cooking spray.

For a softer baked oatmeal: Bake at 350 for 12-15 minutes or until top is just set. Remove from oven (and turn oven off) but cool on top of oven.

For firmer oatmeal squares: Bake at 350 for 15-20 minutes or until top is set and edges are browned. Cool on cooling rack away from oven.

Spot Check: When using steel-cut or old-fashioned oats, increase milk by ½ cup, drop the temperature to 325 degrees. Cook time varies between 35 – 55 minutes, depending on your oven. Oats are done when solid, browned and spoon leaves an indentation.

---

[*] My Version has _____ calories, _____ total carbohydrates, _____ fiber, _____ sugar, _____ protein

Peanut Butter Cookie Baked Protein Oatmeal[*]

Dry Ingredients:

- 1 c. quick oats
- 1/3 c. vanilla or unflavored protein powder
- ½ tsp. baking powder
- A generous pinch of salt
- ½ tsp. cinnamon

Wet Ingredients:

- 1.5 c. milk
- ¼ c. no-calorie sweetener
- 2 eggs, beaten OR ½ c. liquid egg substitute
- ¼ c. PB2 powdered peanut butter

Directions:

Preheat your oven to 350 degrees.

Mix all dry ingredients together in a mixing bowl. Set aside.

Mix together all wet ingredients in another bowl. Add to dry ingredients and combine thoroughly.

Spray an 8 inch x 8 inch baking dish with nonstick cooking spray and pour mixture into it.

For a softer baked oatmeal: Bake at 350 for 12-15 minutes or until top is just set. Remove from oven (and turn oven off) but cool on top of oven.

For firmer oatmeal squares: Bake at 350 for 15-20 minutes or until top is set and edges are browned. Cool on cooling rack away from oven.

Spot Check: When using steel-cut or old-fashioned oats, increase milk by ½ cup, drop the temperature to 325 degrees. Cook time varies between 35 – 55 minutes, depending on your oven. Oats are done when solid, browned and spoon leaves an indentation.

---

[*] My Version has _____ calories, _____ total carbohydrates, _____ fiber, _____ sugar, _____ protein

Maple & Brown Sugar Baked Protein Oatmeal[*]

Dry Ingredients:

- 1 c. quick oats
- 1/3 c. vanilla or unflavored protein powder
- A generous pinch of salt
- ½ tsp. cinnamon

Wet Ingredients:

- 1.5 c. milk
- ¼ c. sugar-free pancake syrup
- 2 eggs, beaten OR ½ c. liquid egg substitute
- ¼ c. Torani Brown Sugar Cinnamon Syrup (see "where to buy" on pg. 143 but in the absence of this ingredient you can use either a ¼ c. brown sugar substitute with the dry ingredients or Splenda Brown Sugar Blend with the dry ingredients but be warned: Splenda Brown Sugar blend has some real sugar in it.)

Optional: Additional sweetener, to taste

Directions:

Preheat your oven to 350 degrees.

Mix all dry ingredients together in a mixing bowl. Set aside.

Mix together all wet ingredients in another bowl. Add to dry ingredients and combine thoroughly.

Spray an 8 inch x 8 inch baking dish with nonstick cooking spray and pour mixture into it.

For a softer baked oatmeal: Bake at 350 for 12-15 minutes or until top is just set. Remove from oven (and turn oven off) but cool on top of oven.

For firmer oatmeal squares: Bake at 350 for 15-20 minutes or until top is set and edges are browned. Cool on cooling rack away from oven.

Spot Check: When using steel-cut or old-fashioned oats, increase milk by ½ cup, drop the temperature to 325 degrees. Cook time varies between 35 – 55 minutes, depending on your oven. Oats are done when solid, browned and spoon leaves an indentation.

---

[*] My Version has _____ calories, _____ total carbohydrates, _____ fiber, _____ sugar, _____ protein

Berry Burst Baked Protein Oatmeal[*]

Dry Ingredients:

- 1 c. quick oats
- 1/3 c. vanilla or unflavored protein powder
- A generous pinch of salt

Wet Ingredients:

- 1.5 c. milk
- ¼ c. no-calorie sweetener
- 2 eggs, beaten OR ½ c. liquid egg substitute
- 1 tsp. vanilla extract

Chunky Stuff:

- 1 – 1 ½ c. mixed berries

Directions:

Preheat your oven to 350 degrees.

Mix all dry ingredients together in a mixing bowl. Set aside.

Mix together all wet ingredients in another bowl. Add to dry ingredients and combine thoroughly. Add chunky stuff and mix again.

Spray an 8 inch x 8 inch baking dish with nonstick cooking spray and pour mixture into it.

For a softer baked oatmeal: Bake at 350 for 12-15 minutes or until top is just set. Remove from oven (and turn oven off) but cool on top of oven.

For firmer oatmeal squares: Bake at 350 for 15-20 minutes or until top is set and edges are browned. Cool on cooling rack away from oven.

Spot Check: When using steel-cut or old-fashioned oats, increase milk by ½ cup, drop the temperature to 325 degrees. Cook time varies between 35 – 55 minutes, depending on your oven. Oats are done when solid, browned and spoon leaves an indentation.

---

[*] My Version has _____ calories, _____ total carbohydrates, _____ fiber, _____ sugar, _____ protein

Oatmeal Raisin Cookie Baked Protein Oatmeal[*]

Dry Ingredients:

- 1.5 c. quick oats
- 1/8 tsp. salt
- 1/3 c. no-calorie sweetener (I used Splenda)

Wet Ingredients:

- ¼ c. Brown Sugar Cinnamon syrup (in the absence of that the same amount of sugar-free pancake syrup + ½ tsp. of cinnamon will do)
- 1.5 c. milk
- 2 eggs, beaten OR ½ cup liquid egg substitute
- ¼ c. vanilla or unflavored protein powder
- 1/3 c. raisins, rinsed of any sugar coating

Optional: Additional sweetener, to taste

Directions:

Preheat your oven to 350 degrees.

In a bowl, mix together the oats, salt and sweetener.

In another bowl combine syrup, cinnamon, milk, eggs and protein powder and mix with a whisk until thoroughly combined (there should be no protein powder lumps).

Pour liquid mixture into the oat mixture and stir well. Finally, stir in raisins and mix through. Spray an 8 inch x 8 inch baking dish with nonstick cooking spray and pour mixture into it.

For a softer baked oatmeal: Bake at 350 for 12-15 minutes or until top is just set. Remove from oven (and turn oven off) but cool on top of oven.

For firmer oatmeal squares: Bake at 350 for 15-20 minutes or until top is set and edges are browned. Cool on cooling rack away from oven.

Spot Check: When using steel-cut or old-fashioned oats, increase milk by ½ cup, drop the temperature to 325 degrees. Cook time varies between 35 – 55 minutes, depending on your oven. Oats are done when solid, browned and spoon leaves an indentation.

---

[*] My Version has _____ calories, _____ total carbohydrates, _____ fiber, _____ sugar, _____ protein

Chapter Four:
Yo!(gurt)...and other dairy things

Yes, yogurt. And cottage cheese. And maybe even a little cream cheese!

You might not think there's much to say about yogurt, but there is! Like I said in the introduction, yogurt had the benefit of calcium, live beneficial bacteria and protein. But it also makes a great base to do other things.

That's what we'll discuss in this chapter.

For some of these recipes you'll need a few supplies, where noted, including:

- Ramekins (depending on how much you can eat you can get either two, three or four ounce ramekins)
- Parfait cups (although a clear plastic disposable cup works just as well!)

As I said in the introduction to this book, you may or may not like Greek yogurt. There many more choices for Greek yogurt now than there were when I was a new post-op. There are many flavored varieties without a lot of added sugar or sugar substitutes and they come in a range of sizes to suit many needs. This is not a pitch for Greek yogurt per se, but just to say that if you'd like to give it a try for its nutritional benefits (higher protein) and texture benefits (creamy, thick texture even with nonfat varieties) there's a lot to choose from.

But what if you absolutely don't want to eat Greek yogurt? That's fine! There are also many regular yogurt offerings. Here's my recommendation on what to look for:

- I personally would not purchase a yogurt that has more than 100 calories per serving. If you see a yogurt that does, that usually means it has either a lot of fat or a lot of sugar in it. Read the label!
- If you don't like fat-free yogurt, there are plenty of 1 or 2% milk fat options

- Beware the "fruit on the bottom" yogurts! They are usually very high in sugar, which could upset your system.
- While any yogurt is going to have some sugar and carbs in it (yogurt is, after all, made from milk, which has a considerable amount of natural sugar – lactose – which contributes to its overall carb count), it shouldn't be over the top. I was always told up to 9g of sugar in a serving of yogurt (that isn't added sugar but, again, lactose) is acceptable but what I'm going to tell you is to ask your registered dietician – and then follow their guidelines!

Cheesecake Yogurt[*]

This is the base for many other things I do with yogurt so I'm listing it as a stand-alone recipe.

Ingredients:

- 1 tbsp. low-fat cream cheese (you can also use the same amount of sugar-free cheesecake flavored pudding mix, dry, but take heed: there will be less fat but more carbs)
- 6 oz. unflavored yogurt (Greek or regular, your choice)
- ½ tsp. lemon juice OR one packet of True Lemon
- 1/8 tsp. pure [K15]vanilla extract
- 1-2 tbsp. of no-calorie sweetener (depending on your preference)
- Optional: ½ scoop (or 1 tbsp.) vanilla or unflavored protein powder

Directions:

If using cream cheese, place it in a microwave safe bowl and microwave it about 10 to 15 seconds or until softened.

Add yogurt, lemon juice, vanilla, and sweetener (if using pudding mix, add it at this point) and mix. Add protein powder at this point also if you intend to use it.

Divide into the appropriate number of servings for you!

Refrigerate unused portions.

---

* My Version has _____ calories, _____ total carbohydrates, _____ fiber, _____ sugar, _____ protein

Strawberry Cheesecake Yogurt Parfait[*]

Ingredients:

- ¼ - ½ c. high fiber cereal, crushed (depending on your eating capacity)
- 1 serving of Cheesecake Yogurt (see pg. 89)
- 1 serving Nik's Strawberry "Quickie Compote" (see pg. 54)

You'll also need: A ramekin, clear plastic cup or a mini-trifle bowl

Directions:

In serving cup, place half the crushed cereal.

On top of that, place half your cheesecake yogurt.

On top of that, place half your strawberry topping.

If this is large enough for you, make another portion the same way, wrap and refrigerate for another time. If you'd like a second layer, repeat.

---

[*] My Version has _____ calories, _____ total carbohydrates, _____ fiber, _____ sugar, _____ protein

Peanut Butter Yogurt[*]

This also makes a dip for fruit!

Ingredients:

- 6 oz. container of unflavored yogurt (Greek or regular, your choice)
- 2 tbsp. powdered peanuts (see "where to buy" on on pg. 143 for brand name and purchasing information)
- 1-2 tbsp. no-calorie sweetener (depending on your preference)
- Optional: ½ scoop (or 1 tbsp.) unflavored or vanilla (or chocolate!) protein powder

Directions:

Mix together yogurt, powdered peanuts, sweetener and protein powder, if using.

Divide into the appropriate number of servings for you!

Refrigerate unused portions.

---

[*] My Version has _____ calories, _____ total carbohydrates, _____ fiber, _____ sugar, _____ protein

PB&J Yogurt Parfait*

Ingredients:

- 1 serving Peanut Butter yogurt (pg. 91)
- ¼ c. sugar-free or no-sugar added jelly, in the flavor of your choosing
- ¼ c. – ½ c. high fiber cereal

You'll also need: A ramekin, clear plastic cup or a mini-trifle bowl

Directions:

In serving cup, place half the crushed cereal.

On top of that place half the peanut butter yogurt.

On top of that place half the jelly.

If this is large enough for you, make another portion the same way, wrap and refrigerate for another time. If you'd like a second layer, repeat.

---

* My Version has _____ calories, _____ total carbohydrates, _____ fiber, _____ sugar, _____ protein

Banana Cream Yogurt[*]

Ingredients:

- 6 oz. container of yogurt (Greek or regular, your choice)
- 1 tbsp. sugar-free banana cream pie dry pudding mix
- 1/8 tsp. pure vanilla extract
- 1-2 tbsp. no-calorie sweetener (depending on your preference)

Directions:

Mix all ingredients together in a bowl, then divide into the appropriate number of servings for you!

Refrigerate unused portions.

---

* My Version has _____ calories, _____ total carbohydrates, _____ fiber, _____ sugar, _____ protein

Banana "Pudding" Yogurt Parfait[*]
Elvis would be so proud!

Ingredients:

- 2 tbsp. finely chopped walnuts
- 2 tbsp. sugar-free pancake syrup
- A pinch of cinnamon
- 1 serving Banana Cream Yogurt (pg. 93)
- ½ - ¼ c. high fiber cereal (depending on your eating capacity)

Directions:

In a bowl, mix walnuts, syrup and cinnamon. Stir to combine and microwave about 10 seconds.

In your container, put half the walnut mixture.

On top of that, place half the Banana Cream yogurt.

On top of that, place half the high fiber cereal.

If this is large enough for you, make another portion the same way, wrap and refrigerate for another time. If you'd like a second layer, repeat.

---

[*] My Version has _____ calories, _____ total carbohydrates, _____ fiber, _____ sugar, _____ protein

Make Your Own "Fruit on the Bottom" Cups[*]

This recipe yields about five half-cup servings that you'd put in small containers (like plastic cups) and cover for quick breakfasts during the week.

Ingredients:

- 20 oz. unflavored yogurt (Greek or regular, your choice!)
- ¼ c. no-calorie sweetener (or to taste)
- 2 tsp. pure vanilla extract
- 1 ¼ c. sugar-free or no sugar added jelly in the flavor of your choice

Directions:

Mix sweetener and vanilla extract directly into yogurt container (if it's too messy use a mixing bowl).

Set out five containers that hold at least ½ c. serving each.

Distribute ¼ c. jelly into each of the cups.

Distribute half a cup of yogurt into each cup.

Cover and refrigerate until ready to use.

_____

* My Version has _____ calories, _____ total carbohydrates, _____ fiber, _____ sugar, _____ protein

Ranch Yogurt[*]

This is one of the few recipes where I strongly recommend Greek yogurt. I'll tell you what to do with it in a moment, although if you like it as is or simply as a dip for a vegetable (if you can eat vegetables), go for it!

Ingredients:

- 6 oz. container Greek yogurt
- 1 heaping tbsp. dry ranch dressing mix

Directions:

Mix all ingredients in a bowl, cover and refrigerate.

---

* My Version has _____ calories, _____ total carbohydrates, _____ fiber, _____ sugar, _____ protein

"Breakfast on the Ranch" Taco Yogurt Parfait[*]

No, I'm not kidding! Nobody ever said a parfait has to be sweet. This is a great way to use up leftovers and have something unconventional for breakfast. For more "un-breakfast" ideas, turn to pg. 111!

Ingredients:

- 1/8 – ¼ c. (depending on your eating capacity) leftover taco meat
- 1/8 – ¼ c. (depending on your eating capacity) Ranch Greek yogurt (pg. 96)
- 1/8 – ¼ c. (depending on your eating capacity) salsa
- 2 tbsp. Mexican shredded cheese
- Optional (but very good!): 1 egg, scrambled, or equivalent amount liquid egg substitute scrambled.

Directions:

In container, place half the taco meat.

On top of that, place half the Ranch Greek yogurt.

On top of that, place half your salsa and one tablespoon of cheese.

On top of that place half your scrambled egg. NOTE: Make sure it's hot when you add it. The hot/cold combo can actually be very good!

If this is enough food for you, use the other half to make another portion, cover and refrigerate it.

If you'd like a second layer repeat with the remainder of the ingredients.

---

* My Version has _____ calories, _____ total carbohydrates, _____ fiber, _____ sugar, _____ protein

11 Things to do with Cottage Cheese

Cottage cheese sometimes gets a bad rap. But it would like you to know a few things about itself.

- Per serving it has a *lot* of protein! One half-cup serving has a whopping 14 grams.
- Yes, it has a tangy flavor and that can be used to your benefit!
- It doesn't *have* to be sweet. Cottage cheese works with savory stuff too!

Armed with this information, let's explore 11 things you can do with cottage cheese: six are sweet, five are savory – one is a submission from a Bariatric Foodie reader! This collection is by no means exhaustive!

If you figure out something great and innovative to do with cottage cheese, by all means share it with the world! Email it to bariatricfoodie@yahoo.com. I'd love to feature you!

Cannoli Cottage Cheese[*]

Ingredients:

- ¼ - ½ c. low-fat cottage cheese (depending on your eating capacity)
- 1 – 2 tbsp. (depending on how much cottage cheese you use) sugar-free Italian Sweet Cream flavored coffee creamer (see "where to buy" on pg. 143)
- ¼ tsp. lemon juice OR half a packet of True Lemon
- A pinch of cinnamon
- 1/8 oz. crushed high fiber or protein-enhanced cereal
- Optional: 6 or 7 sugar-free chocolate chips

Directions:

Combine cottage cheese, creamer, lemon and cinnamon in a blender and blend until curds are totally broken (will slightly resemble ricotta cheese).

Serve in a glass and top with cereal and, if using, chocolate chips.

---

[*] My Version has _____ calories, _____ total carbohydrates, _____ fiber, _____ sugar, _____ protein

Sweet 'n Salty Cottage cheese*

Ingredients:

- ¼ - ½ c. low-fat cottage cheese (depending on your eating capacity)
- 1 – 2 tbsp. no-calorie sweetener, or to taste
- 1 – 2 tbsp. sugar-free, no-calorie caramel syrup, like Torani or Davinci (see "where to buy" on pg. 143)
- Topping: 2 tbsp. chopped pecans, a few sprays of no or low-calorie butter spray, a generous pinch of salt

Directions:

Mix together cottage cheese, sweetener and syrup in a bowl. Set aside.

Set a very small skillet atop a medium flame and allow it to get hot. Add pecans directly (don't use nonstick cooking spray). Toast until they just start to become fragrant, about one to two minutes. Remove from heat.

As the nuts are cooling, spray with butter spray and sprinkle on salt, then toss the nuts in the pan to coat them.

Top cottage cheese with nutty topping.

---

* My Version has _____ calories, _____ total carbohydrates, _____ fiber, _____ sugar, _____ protein

Pumpkin Cheesecake Cottage Cheese[*]

Ingredients:

- 1 tbsp. low-fat cream cheese
- ¼ - ½ c. low-fat cottage cheese (depending on your eating capacity)
- 2 tbsp. pumpkin puree (not pumpkin pie filling)
- 1-2 tbsp. no-calorie sweetener, to taste
- A pinch of pumpkin pie spice
- Optional: High fiber and/or protein-enhanced cereal

Directions:

In a microwave-safe bowl, heat cream cheese for about 15 seconds on high.

Add cottage cheese to blender with cream cheese, pumpkin puree, sweetener and pumpkin pie spice and pulse until curds are completely broken.

Top with cereal, if using.

---

* My Version has _____ calories, _____ total carbohydrates, _____ fiber, _____ sugar, _____ protein

Roasted Pear & Caramel Cottage Cheese[*]
(Look for a remix of this recipe in the "Un-Breakfast" section on pg. 114)

Ingredients:

- 2 slices of a ripened Anjou pear, cut about ¼" in thickness
- A few sprays no or low-calorie butter spray
- 1-2 tbsp. sliced almonds
- ½ - ¼ c. low-fat cottage cheese (depending on your eating capacity)
- 1 – 2 tbsp. sugar-free no-calorie caramel syrup (see "where to buy" on pg. 143)

Optional: Additional no-calorie sweetener, to taste

For this recipe you will also need a grill pan.

Directions:

Set a grill pan over medium heat and allow it to get hot. Spray pear slices with butter spray on both sides. Grill until pear becomes soft and has appropriate grill marks (if you are a visual eater!). Let pears cool then dice them in any size you like.

Add almonds to the pan and toast until they just become fragrant.

In a bowl, combine cottage cheese, sweetener (if using) and caramel syrup and mix well.

Top with grilled diced pears and toasted almonds.

---

* My Version has _____ calories, _____ total carbohydrates, _____ fiber, _____ sugar, _____ protein

Ambrosia Cottage Cheese[*]
(Makes 2 – 4 servings, depending on your eating capacity)

Ingredients:

- ½ c. low-fat cottage
- 1 tbsp. sugar-free, no-calorie Davinci Toasted Marshmallow flavored syrup (see "where to buy" on pg. 143)
- ½ scoop (or 1 tbsp.) vanilla or unflavored protein powder
- 1 – 2 fresh pineapple chunks, minced
- 1 – 2 mandarin orange wedges, de-seeded
- 1 tbsp. unsweetened shredded coconut (see "where to buy" on pg. 143)

Directions:

In a bowl, mix together cottage cheese, syrup and protein powder.

Add the remainder of the ingredients and stir well.

If this yields than one serving for you, wrap unused portion and refrigerate until ready to eat.

---

[*] My Version has _____ calories, _____ total carbohydrates, _____ fiber, _____ sugar, _____ protein

Reader Submission: Cheryl's Cherry Cheesecake Cottage Cheese[*]

Ingredients:

- ½ c. low-fat cottage cheese
- No-calorie sweetener, to taste
- 1/3 c. sugar-free cherry pie filling
- ½ of a Graham cracker crushed

Directions:

Combine cottage cheese and sweetener in a bowl.

Top with pie filling, then with graham cracker.

---

[*] My Version has _____ calories, _____ total carbohydrates, _____ fiber, _____ sugar, _____ protein

Greek Cottage Cheese[*]

Ingredients:

- ½ - ¼ c. low-fat cottage cheese (depending on your eating capacity)
- ½ - 1 tbsp. (depending on how much cottage cheese you use) feta cheese
- 1 tbsp. diced tomato
- 1 tbsp. peeled and diced cucumber
- 1 tbsp. sliced Kalamata olives
- Salt and pepper, to taste

Directions:

Combine all ingredients in a bowl and mix well.

If this yields more than one serving for you, cover and refrigerate unused portion until ready to eat!

---

* My Version has _____ calories, _____ total carbohydrates, _____ fiber, _____ sugar, _____ protein

Bacon Bleu Cheese Cottage Cheese[*]

Ingredients:

- 1 Laughing Cow Light blue cheese flavored wedge
- ½ - ¼ c. low-fat cottage cheese (depending on your eating capacity)
- 1 tbsp. bacon bits OR ½ a slice of cooked bacon, crumbled
- Optional: 1 tbsp. diced tomatoes, a pinch of shredded Iceberg lettuce

Directions:

In a microwave-safe bowl, heat cheese wedge about 10 seconds.

Mix in cottage cheese and thoroughly combine. Then mix in bacon bits.

Top with tomato and lettuce, if desired.

---

* My Version has _____ calories, _____ total carbohydrates, _____ fiber, _____ sugar, _____ protein

Italian Cottage Cheese*

Ingredients:

- ¼ - ½ c. low-fat cottage cheese (depending on your eating capacity)
- 1 tbsp. grated Parmesan cheese
- Freshly ground black pepper, to taste
- ¼ c. warmed spaghetti sauce
- 2 tbsp. shredded part-skim mozzarella cheese

Directions:

In a small blender (like a Magic Bullet, etc.), pulse cottage cheese until curds have completely broken up. Transfer to a small bowl.

Add cheese and pepper and mix thoroughly.

Top with warmed spaghetti sauce and shredded cheese. Allow the warm sauce to melt the cheese.

---

* My Version has _____ calories, _____ total carbohydrates, _____ fiber, _____ sugar, _____ protein

Fiesta Cottage Cheese[*]

Ingredients:

- 1 Laughing Cow Light Queso Fresco Chipotle cheese wedge
- ¼ - ½ c. low-fat cottage cheese (depending on your eating capacity)
- 1 – 2 tbsp. salsa (depending on how much cottage cheese used)
- 1 – 2 tbsp. black beans (great use for leftovers!)

Directions:

In a microwave-safe bowl, heat cheese wedge 10 seconds on high.

Add cottage cheese and mix thoroughly.

Add remaining ingredients and mix thoroughly.

---

* My Version has _____ calories, _____ total carbohydrates, _____ fiber, _____ sugar, _____ protein

"Fancy Pants" Cottage Cheese[*]

I named this dish the way I did because I really did feel like it was dressing up cottage cheese! But hey…we deserve fancy food too, right?

Ingredients:

- 1 Garlic & Herb flavored Laughing Cow Light cheese wedge
- ¼ c – ½ c. cottage cheese (depending on your eating capacity)
- 1 tbsp. onion, cut into slivers
- 1 tbsp. sliced button mushrooms
- A few sprays of low or no-calorie butter spray
- 2 tbsp. balsamic vinegar
- Salt and fresh-ground black pepper, to taste

Directions:

In a microwave-safe bowl, heat cheese wedge for 10 – 15 seconds or until softened.

Add cottage cheese and mix thoroughly.

Spray a small skillet generously with non-stick cooking spray, set it over medium heat and allow it to get hot. Sauté onions and mushrooms until onions turn light brown and mushrooms have reduced in size. Spray with butter spray as you are cooking.

When onions and mushrooms are done cooking, add balsamic vinegar and cook for about two more minutes, allowing it to reduce.

Spot Check: Warning for visual eaters: the Balsamic vinegar will probably make your onions a reddish color.

Top cottage cheese mixture with onion/mushroom mixture and salt and pepper, if desired.

---

[*] My Version has _____ calories, _____ total carbohydrates, _____ fiber, _____ sugar, _____ protein

Chapter Five:
"Un-Breakfasts"

You know you don't *have* to eat traditional breakfast dishes for breakfast. You don't even have to eat traditional breakfast food for breakfast.

This section celebrates "un-breakfast," which, in my estimation, falls into two categories:

1. Meals that are inspired by breakfast foods but can work any time of day.
2. Meals that you can eat for breakfast that don't even resemble breakfast, but still have the nutrients you need to get up and go!

I just want to make one distinction. Un-breakfast isn't (necessarily) brunch. There are plenty of recipes in this book that have a "brunch-y" feel, like the frittatas and the egg casseroles, even the baked oatmeal. Rather, the un-breakfast is the practice of thinking outside the box.

To that end, I offer up a few recipes and leave you to be inspired by them. If you come up with anything good, email me at bariatricfoodie@yahoo.com. I'd love to hear what you're cooking!

...But first, what makes a good breakfast?

Having completely failed, at the beginning of this book, to figure out why we eat the breakfast foods we eat, I decided to shift my focus. I instead set out to figure out exactly what overall rules govern a good breakfast. I was thinking not in terms of specific foods (eggs are good, pizza is bad, etc.) but of overarching principles (perhaps many carbs and a little protein or vice versa...).

So here's what I have for you. This is pulled from a lot of reading and while there are many thoughts, these seemed to be universal. Still I hesitate to call it a rule so I will say that it is my strong opinion that, based on research, breakfast should:

1. Contain foods from the major macro-nutrient groups. Translation: there should be some carbs, there should be some protein, and there should be some fat. Don't cut any of these out of the equation.

2. Breakfast need not be a large meal. In fact, many sources say it's better that it isn't. Most dietary experts are now advocating small mini—meals throughout the day so this makes sense. If you eat a huge breakfast you're unlikely to eat for a *long* time after. Besides, depending on your schedule you may not need all those calories and what does the body do with ingested calories it does not need...?

3. Experts also agree that you shouldn't eat breakfast until you actually have an appetite. It actually said until you are hungry but in our world that may never happen. I define appetite as the will and the willing*ness* to eat. Even if you don't feel ravenous, you know that point where you know your body needs nutrition and you are physically able to accommodate that need.

So...having solved absolutely *nothing*, let's forge into the world of unbreakfast. Some of these dishes have traditional breakfast foods in them, some of them don't. They all have a good balance of nutrients to get your day started. Some of them are even good grab 'n go meals.

C'mon! Let's explore.

Cajun Stuffed Baby 'Bellas[*]

Ingredients:

- 4 – 6 baby Portabella mushrooms
- 2 oz. Andouille sausage, casing removed
- 2 inches of a zucchini, diced
- 2 tbsp. onion, finely diced
- ¼ jalapeno pepper, chopped (and seeded if you don't want it to be spicy)½ tsp. Cajun seasoning
- ¼ c. shredded cheese blend of your choice
- Salt & pepper, to taste

Directions:

Preheat oven to 350 degrees.

Quickly rinse mushrooms and pat dry. Place them in a baking dish, stem side up. Use a small paring knife to remove stems.

Set a skillet over medium heat and allow it to get hot. Add sausage and break up with a spatula. Once meat is slightly browned, add zucchini and onion, stirring into the meat.

Cook until meat is completely done, then add jalapeno and Cajon seasoning. Drain mixture if necessary.

Fill mushroom cavities with sausage mixture. Sprinkle with cheese.

Bake for 10 to 12 minutes or until mushrooms have softened and cheese is completely melted.

---

* My Version has _____ calories, _____ total carbohydrates, _____ fiber, _____ sugar, _____ protein

Roasted Pear with Ricotta Nut Topping[*]

Don't be put off by the savory/sweet nature of this dish. The two tastes play off each other wonderfully. You'll be surprised how satisfying this dish is!

Ingredients:

- 1 pear, peeled, seeded and cored (Bosc or Bartlett pears work well)
- ½ tbsp. extra-virgin olive oil
- 1 wedge Laughing Cow Light white cheddar cheese
- ¼ c. ricotta cheese
- 1 small basil leaf, finely chopped (if using dried basil, a small pinch will do)
- 2 tbsp. sliced almonds
- 1 tbsp. sugar-free caramel syrup (the kind used for topping ice cream)

Directions:

Preheat your oven to 425 degrees.

Set a skillet or a grill pan over medium heat and allow it to get hot.

Brush the cut sides of the pear halves with oil and place them on the pan. Cook about 2-3 minutes or until cut side has softened slightly and grill marks appear. Place in a baking dish and bake for 10 minutes or until softened. Set aside to cool when done. Wash and dry skillet and set aside.

While the pear is baking, place white cheddar cheese in a microwave-safe bowl and cook 15to 20 seconds, or until melted. Add ricotta cheese and basil and mix well.

Set a dry skillet (can be the same skillet used to cook pear, after washing and drying) over medium heat and allow it to get hot. Add almond slices and toss about one minute or until nuts darken slightly and become fragrant.

Assemble the dish by place the cooked and cooled pear on a plate. Fill the cavity (made by coring and peeling the pear) with the ricotta/cheese mixture. Drizzle with caramel sauce and top with almond slices.

Spot Check: If a half-pear is too much for you to handle, check out pg. 102 for a softer variation of this recipe!

---

[*] My Version has _____ calories, _____ total carbohydrates, _____ fiber, _____ sugar, _____ protein

Breakfast Chili[*]

Chili is one of those foods I can almost universally say is a post-op favorite. It delivers protein, it's easy to eat and it's customizable enough for people to "do their own thing" with it.

This is a great make-ahead breakfast. It can also make a good sit-down breakfast for a weekend. Either way, play with the recipe – make it yours!

Ingredients:

- 4 eggs (or equivalent amount liquid egg substitute)
- 1 small onion, diced
- 1 green pepper, diced
- 1 tsp. garlic, minced
- 8 oz. breakfast sausage (whatever meat, or vegetarian substitute, you like)
- 4 slices cooked bacon, broken into bits
- 12 oz. black beans, drained and rinsed
- 16 oz. petite diced tomatoes (if you'd like a mild flavor) or tomatoes & chiles (if you'd like a spicier flavor)
- 1 packet of chili seasoning (or 1.25 oz. of your favorite chili seasoning)
- 2 tbsp. tomato paste
- ¾ c. water
- Optional toppings: Unflavored Greek yogurt, shredded cheese, red onions, sliced olives or anything else you like!

Directions:

Spray a large skillet with nonstick cooking spray, set it over medium heat and allow it to get hot.

Scramble the eggs until completely done. Set aside.

Spray a pot or a deep skillet with nonstick cooking spray, set it over medium heat and allow it to get hot. Add onions and green pepper and sauté about two minutes or until vegetables soften. Add garlic and stir.

Add sausage meat and break up with a spatula as if browning ground meat. Cook until meat is fully browned. Drain off excess fat, if necessary.

Add bacon bits, beans, tomatoes, seasoning and water, stir and bring the mixture to a boil. Reduce heat and simmer about 30 minutes. In the last 10 minutes of cooking, add scrambled eggs and stir to distribute throughout.

---

[*] My Version has _____ calories, _____ total carbohydrates, _____ fiber, _____ sugar, _____ protein

Divide into appropriate sized portions and refrigerate until ready to use.

You can also put your own spin on Breakfast Chili by switching up the kind of meat you use. Try one of these suggestions – or something of your own imagining!

- Make your Breakfast Chili Mexican by using turkey chorizo sausage
- Make your Breakfast Chili Italian by using turkey Italian sausage
- Make your Breakfast Chili Cajun, by using Andouille

Nik's Scotch Egg[*]

No…this is not an egg with Scotch in it, but thanks for thinking that! I didn't make up this recipe (many of you probably already know that). I first heard about this where I hear about many new recipes – Food Network! I'm glad I did. It seems like a perfect little protein-packed meal and it was relatively easy to test it! Special thanks to my dear friend Julia for converting and testing this recipe!

Ingredients:

- 6 large eggs
- 1 lb. lean turkey sausage meat
- 2 tbsp. unflavored Greek yogurt
- 2 tbsp. Dijon mustard
- 1 tsp. parsley or parsley flakes
- ½ c. Parmesan cheese (can be fresh grated if you like) + ¼ c. Parmesan cheese (powdered kind)
- Salt and pepper, to taste

Directions:

Preheat your oven to 400 degrees.

Bring a pot of water to a boil. With a slotted spoon, carefully insert eggs into the water and cook for two minutes. Drain from boiling water and rinse with cold water. Set aside.

Spot Check: Because you will be putting the eggs in the oven, you want to start with a soft-boiled egg.

In a bowl, combine sausage, yogurt, mustard and parsley and mix well with your hands.

Once eggs are thoroughly cooled, crack and peel them.

Place the quarter-cup of store-bought parmesan cheese on a plate. Dredge eggs in it until well coated.

Spot Check: We dredge the eggs in the Parmesan to absorb the moisture on the outside of the egg white. Using Parmesan instead of flour reduces the carbohydrate count.

Divide meat into six equal sized "meatballs." One by one, flatten a meatball into a large round disc in the palm of your hand. Place the egg in the middle of it and wrap the sausage around the egg.

---

* My Version has _____ calories, _____ total carbohydrates, _____ fiber, _____ sugar, _____ protein

Spot Check: If you find it difficult to wrap the sausage around the egg, use a butter knife to spread the sausage around the egg but make sure there are no holes!

Place remaining cheese in a bowl and toss each egg in the cheese to coat.

Place a draining rack inside a baking pan and put all the eggs on the rack. Bake them for 15 to 20 minutes or until the sausage is cooked and the cheese has slightly browned.

Spot Check: This recipe probably works best with people with heartier appetites and those who can handle things like reduced-fat meatballs.

NOTE: If this portion is too big for you, skip the egg and make a sausage meatball. Just form the sausage into meatballs of desired size, toss in the Parmesan cheese and bake for the same amount of time.

Fun Variations

Here are a few ideas on how to play with this concept. Simply use the below substitutions with the amount of Greek yogurt listed in the original recipe. You can omit the mustard and parsley. If you are using sausage links, make sure to remove the casings before mixing the meat.

- Make your Scotch Egg Mexican by using turkey chorizo sausage
- Make your Scotch Egg Italian by using turkey Italian sausage
- Make your Scotch Egg Cajun, by using Andouille

Sausage & Lentil Breakfast Soup[*]

This is another make-ahead recipe that's especially good in the winter! Invest in some good, microwave-safe food storage bowls. This also freezes well, especially if you have a wet/dry food vacuum sealer. Otherwise, I'd advise you to put this soup in a zip-top freezer storage bag and pressing out as much air as you can.

Ingredients:

- 16 oz. breakfast sausage (can either be the kind you cut into patties or links, but cut the casings off!)
- 1 small onion, diced
- 1 small yellow squash, diced (you can remove the skins if they bother you)
- 1 small zucchini, diced (you can remove the skins if they bother you)
- 15 oz. chicken or vegetable broth
- 2 tsp. minced garlic
- 1 lb. dry lentils
- 10 oz. can petite diced tomatoes
- Salt and pepper, to taste
- Optional: A pinch of cayenne pepper (if you like spicy food), a pinch of sage (bumps up the sausage flavor), 1 tsp. Cajun seasoning (or, if it's available in your grocery store, swap out Andouille sausage for your breakfast sausage for a fun twist!)

Directions:

Set a deep skillet over medium heat and allow it to get hot. Add breakfast sausage and brown like you would ground beef.

Add vegetables and garlic and sauté about two minutes. If necessary, drain any excess fat.

Add chicken broth, dry lentils and tomatoes. Stir and taste. Add seasonings, taste and adjust.

Spot Check: My rule of thumb with seasoning is that when you taste something that's not fully cooked that you've seasoned, it should be just ever so slightly under-seasoned. Cooking things intensifies seasonings. If you need more you can always add more, but it's really hard to take over-seasoning away!

---

[*] My Version has _____ calories, _____ total carbohydrates, _____ fiber, _____ sugar, _____ protein

Bring the mixture to a boil, stirring every few moments, then drop the heat down to low and cover. Cook for 30 to 40 minutes or until lentils are fully cooked, stirring occasionally.

Spot Check: If it's easier on your stomach, take an immersion blender to this recipe and make it pureed! This *may* make it work in a pureed phase diet, but check with your nutritionist or registered dietician to be sure.

Stuffed Avocado[*]

Ingredients:

- ½ of avocado, seed removed, and flesh diced small (NOTE: leave skin intact and reserve)
- 2 tbsp. salsa (NOTE: Fresh is especially good but jarred is also fine)
- 1 oz. tiny shrimp OR 2 full-sized cooked shrimp, cut into small pieces
- 1/8 tsp. minced garlic
- 1 tsp. lemon juice
- 1 tbsp. unflavored Greek yogurt

Directions:

In a bowl, toss together avocado, salsa, shrimp, garlic and lemon juice.

Add Greek yogurt and mix thoroughly.

Spoon mixture back into avocado skin. Chill until ready to serve.

Spot Check: If there is too much filling, you can use the extra atop some savory Greek yogurt or cottage cheese OR you can use part of the other half of the avocado to make another portion! Also note, when storing the remaining avocado (preferably in the refrigerator in a zip-top storage back) be sure to put the seed in there with the remaining half – it helps slow the ripening process!

---

[*] My Version has _____ calories, _____ total carbohydrates, _____ fiber, _____ sugar, _____ protein

Protein Power Balls[*]

Ingredients:

- 1 c. high fiber cereal, crushed into crumbs
- 1 scoop vanilla protein powder
- ¼ tsp cinnamon
- 1 tbsp. natural peanut butter
- 2 tbsp. peanut flour (see "Where to Buy" on pg. 143)
- 3-4 tbsp. milk
- Optional: Splenda or other no-calorie sweetener, to taste

Directions:

Combine cereal crumbs, protein powder, peanut flour, cinnamon and sweetener (if using) in a bowl. Mix well.

In a microwave-safe cup or bowl, microwave peanut butter for 15-30 seconds, until liquefied. Add to the dry mixture.

Add milk, one tablespoon at a time, until the scoops of the mixture will hold together.

Use a tablespoon to scoop out heaps of the mixture and form it into balls.

Refrigerate until ready to serve.

Spot Check: Although these don't last long in my house, they can be stored in an airtight container or zip-top storage bag, in the refrigerator, for up to a week.

---

* My Version has _____ calories, _____ total carbohydrates, _____ fiber, _____ sugar, _____ protein

Reader Submission: Sue's Quinoa Salad with Black Beans and Avocado *

Ingredients:

- 1 c. quinoa
- 1 tbsp. olive oil
- 1 ¾ cups water
- 1 (16 oz.) cans black beans, drained and rinsed
- 1 avocado, chopped into chunks
- ¾ c. cherry tomatoes, quartered- I use a whole container
- ½ a red onion, diced
- 1 tsp. garlic, minced
- 1 red bell pepper, cut into chunks
- 1 English cucumber, diced
- ½ c. cilantro, rough chopped
- The juice of one lime (if you like extra tang, also use the juice of one lemon)
- ½ tsp. ground cumin
- ½ tbsp. olive oil

Directions:

Set a medium sauce pan over medium heat and allow it to get hot. Add olive oil and spread around pan before adding quinoa and toast for about 2-3 minutes until it starts to smell nutty.

Spot Check: If you prefer your quinoa rinsed (un-rinsed quinoa can sometimes be bitter), make sure to drain it well before adding it to the oil.

Add water, stir once, cover, and simmer with a lid for 20 minutes.

While quinoa is cooking, prepare all other ingredients. Prepare dressing by combining the lime juice, oil, cumin, and salt. Whisk vigorously. Taste and adjust seasoning as necessary.

When the quinoa is finished, remove from heat and fluff with a fork.

Spot Check: An easy way to tell if quinoa is finished is when a small ring pops out of each seed. In general, quinoa cooks up firmer than rice, so don't expect it to be soft but it should not be crunch either!

Add black beans and toss to warm through.

Let the quinoa cool for about 5 minutes and then add all the remaining ingredients, including dressing, then mix well.

Taste again and adjust seasoning. Can be served hot or cold.

---

* My Version has _____ calories, _____ total carbohydrates, _____ fiber, _____ sugar, _____ protein

Chapter Six:
Breakfast Protein Drinks

I would be remiss not to include a few breakfast-themed protein shakes. Many of us start our day with a good old protein drink for many reasons.

For me, a protein drink was always my first meal because I couldn't handle solid food in the morning. But as time wore on, my system changed. And now that I know not to eat breakfast until I actually have an appetite, it's even easier to consume food at breakfast (although still not that much).

The big thing I want you to remember is this. It's important to start your day with *good nutrition*. That nutrition does not have to be solid food! A protein shake can contain a good balance of great nutrients to get your day going strong and be kinder and gentler to your tummy!

There are five ideas in this section. If you'd like more ideas, I encourage you to check out another of my books, The Bariatric Foodie Guide to Perfect Protein Shakes. See the "Where to Buy" section (pg. 143) for details on ordering.

Bloody Mary Protein Mocktail[*]

This drink is for those who appreciated a nice glass of V-8. The great thing about this drink is that it can be customized to suit your tastes! Here, I am proposing a spicy version but if that's not your thing, nix it! Go with what makes you feel good!

Ingredients:

- 4 oz. no sugar added tomato juice
- 1 scoop unflavored protein powder
- 2 oz. water
- ¼ tsp. Old Bay seasoning (or any seafood seasoning)
- Ice

Directions:

Combine all ingredients except ice in a blender and mix well for about 30-45 seconds.

If you'd like your drink "on the rocks," serve over ice. If you'd like it blended in, add it to the blender after the first blend. Mix until all ice is crushed.

---

* My Version has _____ calories, _____ total carbohydrates, _____ fiber, _____ sugar, _____ protein

Orange Sunrise Protein Drink[*]

Those who already have *The Bariatric Foodie Guide to Perfect Protein Shakes* know this shake as an Orange Creamsicle. Whatever you call it, it's refreshing and good. Perfect start to a summer day!

Ingredients:

- 4 oz. unflavored Greek yogurt
- 2-3 oz. water
- 1 sugar-free orange-flavored drink stick
- 1 serving vanilla protein powder (go by what your protein says is a serving!)
- No-calorie sweetener, to taste
- Ice
- Optional: Take this drink to the next level with a half-cup of frozen berries!

Directions:

Combine all ingredients in your blender and blend until thoroughly mixed.

---

* My Version has _____ calories, _____ total carbohydrates, _____ fiber, _____ sugar, _____ protein

Green God(dess) Protein Drink[*]

Ingredients:

- 1 c. baby spinach
- 1 Granny Smith Apple, seeded and cored (and peeled if fruit skins bother you)
- 5-6 pineapple chunks
- ½ c. unflavored Greek yogurt
- ½ c. cold water
- 1 scoop unflavored protein powder (or vanilla works as well)
- No calorie sweetener, to taste
- Optional: ice

Directions:

Combine all ingredients in a blender and blend!

---

* My Version has _____ calories, _____ total carbohydrates, _____ fiber, _____ sugar, _____ protein

French Toast Hot Protein Drink[*]

Ingredients:

- 4 oz. cold milk (the temperature is important here!)
- 1 serving vanilla protein powder (go by what your protein says is a serving!)
- Either 2 tbsp. sugar-free Torani Brown Sugar Cinnamon flavored syrup (See "Where to Buy" on pg. 143) OR 1 tbsp. sugar-free pancake syrup and a generous pinch of cinnamon
- 1/8 tsp. butter extract (in the grocery store baking aisle – does not add any calories!)
- 8 oz. boiling water
- Optional: Whipped cream for topping along with an additional cinnamon sprinkle

Directions:

In a 16-ounce mug, mix together milk and protein powder. Stir until a thick, lump-free paste forms.

Spot Check: It's really important to not have any lumps in this initial mixture. The final texture of your hot drink depends on it! Any random lumps will turn hard and rubbery when they meet the boiling liquid, so invest the extra minute or two and stir well!

Add the syrup and butter extract and stir again.

Add boiling water slowly while stirring the drink. It may take some practice but this method should eventually yield a smooth, lump-free hot protein drink.

Top with whipped cream, if desired.

Spot Check: Some of you may have heard that heating protein "destroys" it. This is not true! While it is true that it changes the form of the protein (much the way cooking an egg changes an egg) your body can still use the protein. Also, if you have another proven method of making hot protein drinks, don't feel bound by mine! Use whatever method works best for you to get a smooth, lump-free drink.

---

[*] My Version has _____ calories, _____ total carbohydrates, _____ fiber, _____ sugar, _____ protein

Cinnamon Bun Hot Protein Drink[*]

Ingredients:

- 4 oz. cold milk (temperature is important here!)
- 1 serving vanilla protein powder (go by what your protein says is a serving)
- 1 tbsp. sugar-free cheesecake pudding mix
- Either 2 tbsp. sugar-free Torani Brown Sugar Cinnamon flavored syrup (see "Where to Buy" on pg. 143) OR 1 tbsp. sugar-free pancake syrup and a generous pinch of cinnamon
- 8 oz. boiling water
- Optional: Whipped cream with a sprinkle of additional cinnamon for topping

Directions:

In a 16-ounce mug, mix together milk, protein powder and pudding mix. Stir until a thick, lump-free paste forms.

Spot Check: It's really important to not have any lumps in this initial mixture. The final texture of your hot drink depends on it! Any random lumps will turn hard and rubbery when they meet the boiling liquid, so invest the extra minute or two and stir well!

Add the syrup and stir again. Add boiling water slowly while stirring the drink. It may take some practice but this method should eventually yield a smooth, lump-free hot protein drink.

Top with whipped cream, if desired.

Spot Check: Some of you may have heard that heating protein "destroys" it. This is not true! While it is true that it changes the form of the protein (much the way cooking an egg changes an egg) your body can still use the protein. Also, if you have another proven method of making hot protein drinks, don't feel bound by mine! Use whatever method works best for you to get a smooth, lump-free drink.

---

[*] My Version has _____ calories, _____ total carbohydrates, _____ fiber, _____ sugar, _____ protein

Blueberry Muffin Hot Protein Drink[*]

Ingredients:

- 4 oz. cold milk (temperature is important here!)
- 1 serving vanilla protein powder (go by what your protein says is a serving)
- 2 tbsp. sugar-free Davinci Blueberry syrup (see "Where to Buy" on pg. 143)
- 1/8 tsp. butter extract
- 8 oz. boiling water
- No-calorie sweetener, to taste
- Optional: Whipped cream for topping

Directions:

In a 16-ounce mug, mix together milk and protein powder. Stir until a thick, lump-free paste forms.

Spot Check: It's really important to not have any lumps in this initial mixture. The final texture of your hot drink depends on it! Any random lumps will turn hard and rubbery when they meet the boiling liquid, so invest the extra minute or two and stir well!

Add the syrup and butter extract and stir again.

Add boiling water slowly while stirring the drink. It may take some practice but this method should eventually yield a smooth, lump-free hot protein drink.

Top with whipped cream, if desired

Spot Check: Some of you may have heard that heating protein "destroys" it. This is not true! While it is true that it changes the form of the protein (much the way cooking an egg changes an egg) your body can still use the protein. Also, if you have another proven method of making hot protein drinks, don't feel bound by mine! Use whatever method works best for you to get a smooth, lump-free drink.

---

* My Version has _____ calories, _____ total carbohydrates, _____ fiber, _____ sugar, _____ protein

Chapter Seven:
Really, really, really cool resources

Yes, all three "really's" were *really* necessary.

Here are a few resources I've put together to help you play with your food. Use them in respect to these recipes or any recipes you want to try out.

My Recipe Test Kitchen

Some of us (not me) are born with the ability to invent or tweak recipes by instinct. For the rest of us, it's helpful to have a process to use and a way to document the outcome. For those of us who need that, I offer this – the Bariatric Foodie method of testing home recipes. This is a simplified version of the process I used for every single recipe in this book!

This method is meant to be written on a sheet of paper to keep you organized.

Proposed Recipe Name: This is optional but can help if you are trying to remix a recipe. For example, my recipe called "Breakfast Chili" gives a good idea of the flavors I'm going for: chili with a breakfast kick!

Recipe Based on: If your recipe is based on another recipe – as in the Breakfast Chili example where it is based on chili – list it here to keep the spirit of the original recipe in mind.

Proposed Ingredients: List all the ingredients you propose to use and how much of each. If you're not sure how to approach this, a good way to start is to look at a traditional version of a recipe (if you are remixing a recipe) or look at similar recipes (if you are trying to think up a new recipe). Look at the ingredients in the recipe and note where healthier ingredients could be used.

Be sure to include:

- All spices you intend to use
- All liquids (including water) that you intend to use
- All oils you intend to use

Proposed Preparation Directions: Again, inspiration recipes are helpful here. Just make sure to take note where your changes would cause a change in preparation. For example, in cooked recipes, protein powder must either be "tempered" (added to room temperature or cold water before mixed into hot substances) or you should use a protein that is made for cooking. Take note of these things so that you remember to do them when trying out your recipe.

Be sure to include:

- Cooking temperatures if you are baking
- Cook times (how long to boil, sauté, etc.)

Recipe Notes: Make recipe notes as you're trying out the recipe. Take note of anything that surprises you, any questions you have, anything that makes you take pause as you are trying out your recipe. It need not be world-class writing, just make sure you write legibly and in a way that you're likely to understand later.

Be sure to include:

- Your impressions of the final result (Did you like it?)
- Anything having to do with the texture of the recipe (Was it supposed to be moist and it turned out dry or vice versa? Make note of it!)
- Anything about your result that you don't understand. Then come to Bariatric Foodie's Facebook Page and ask questions!

The Bariatric Foodie Sweetener Conversion Guide

Because Splenda® measures cup-for-cup with sugar, those measurements do not appear below, however here are the measurements for the other popular no-calorie sweeteners.

Stevia

Sugar	Stevia Powdered Extract	Stevia liquid concentrate
1 cup	1 teaspoon	1 teaspoon
1 tablespoon	1/4 teaspoon	6 to 9 drops
1 teaspoon	A pinch to 1/16 teaspoons	2 to 4 drops

Equal

Sugar	Equal® Packet	Equal® for Recipes	Equal® Spoonful
2 teaspoons	1 packet	approx. 1/4 teaspoon	2 teaspoons
1 tablespoon	1 1/2 packets	1/2 teaspoon	1 tablespoon
1/4 cup	6 packets	1 3/4 teaspoons	1/4 cup
1/3 cup	8 packets	2 1/2 teaspoons	1/3 cup
1/2 cup	12 packets	3 1/2 teaspoons	1/2 cup
3/4 cup	18 packets	5 1/2 teaspoons	3/4 cup
1 cup	24 packets	7 1/4 teaspoons	1 cup
1 pound	57 packets	5 Tbsp. + 2 tsp.	2 1/4 cups

Sweet'N Low

Sugar	Sweet'N Low Packets	Sweet'N Low Bulk	Sweet'N Low Liquid
1/4 cup granulated sugar	6 packets	2 teaspoons	1 1/2 teaspoons
1/3 cup granulated sugar	8 packets	2 1/2 teaspoons	2 teaspoons
1/2 cup granulated sugar	12 packets	4 teaspoons	1 tablespoon
1 cup granulated sugar	24 packets	8 teaspoons	2 tablespoons

How to Figure Out the Nutrition Information of Any Recipe

It's the most frequent complaint I get on or about Bariatric Foodie. "Why don't you give nutrition information?" I've gone over the reasons earlier in this book but I'll restate that it's mostly for three reasons:

1. The ingredients to which you have access may differ than the ones to which I have access. Further, different ingredients can, and often do, have different nutrition information, even if just by a few grams of something.
2. You are likely to change my recipes to your liking – and that's fine! However, when you change a recipe's ingredients, you change its nutrition information.
3. Those two things being the case, I think it's important that you know how to figure out a recipe's nutrition information for yourself. That way you can decide if a recipe fits into your plan as-is or needs tweaking.

Here's how to figure out the nutrition information for any recipe.

Online method:

Step One: Get to Tracking!!!

Log into (or join) an online food tracker like FitDay, Sparkpeople or LiveStrong. Most of these sites have functions that allow you to make a custom entry into a daily food journal.

Step Two: Don't leave ANYTHING out

Log every single ingredient, even if you don't think it has any caloric value. Include no calorie sweetener and salt as well. Those things are important to your daily intake numbers.

Also be sure to indicate the measurements you actually used.

Step Three: Divide and conquer

Some trackers ask you for the amount of servings your recipe yielded. Some do not. If they do, when you are finished inputting your recipe you simply publish it and the tracker will tell you how many calories, carbs, protein, etc. is in that one serving. If not, when you publish it, the food tracker will give you the stats for the entire recipe. **Do not freak out.** To get the information for just one serving, you'll need to figure out how many servings your recipe yielded.

Don't know? Understandable. Some of us pre-portion our foods and therefore know how many servings a recipe yields and some folks cook it and eat it until it's gone. Neither way is wrong. Here are some tips:

- If you made a casserole, try pre-cutting the casserole into the sized pieces you would eat.
- For stews/soups/chilies, I immediately transfer to a storage container (even if I am serving it that night). I do so with a measuring cup (for me that'd be an eight ounce measuring cup…for you it may be smaller). Do that and count the number of times you ladled it out…and there's your number of portions!

The "Hand Method"

For those that don't want to use a food tracker, you can always do this by hand. It requires a little more time and a bit more diligence about adhering to the portion sizes that the particular food product calls for, though.

Step One:

Take down the nutrition information for each ingredient you used in a recipe (from the nutrition label) and the number of servings of each food you used. Write the amounts down on a piece of paper.

Step Two:

Add up all the various pieces of information (calories, carbohydrates, etc.) from each ingredient to get totals. Again, these totals are for the entire batch you made. Don't freak out!

Step Three:

Divide that number by the number of servings.

In closing I'd like to say once you start paying attention to your nutritional information (and here's a good primer on what to pay attention to), this almost becomes second nature. At four years post-op I can guesstimate, within just a few calories, any recipe I make or eat. It just takes practice.

The Bariatric Foodie Protein Shake Check-Up

So you've found the PERFECT protein shake. You've tested, you've tweaked, you've tested, you've tweaked and now it is divine. And Nik has to come and mess it all up!

It's good, as we're playing with our food, to every once in a while do a "check-up" on our protein shakes (with all our recipes, really) to make sure we're still moving in the right direction.

Why?

Well, protein shakes are tricky things. It's easy for them to tiptoe over the line of being protein-heavy to being carb-heavy. As I've said ad nauseum, carbs are NOT evil. But your protein shake should be predominantly protein. So let's go over how you give YOUR shake a check-up.

The Base

What liquid/soft substances are you using with your base? Some popular ones are water, milk and Greek yogurt. I did hear recently of a post-op who uses a bit of ice cream in their shake. I'll get to that in a moment.

Here are some things to consider:

- What percentage of fat is in my shake base? If you're using whole milk that could tip the balance of your shake toward being more fat than protein, depending on other ingredients.
- How many carbs are in my base? Milk has 12 grams of carbs. That's fine so long as you're watching your carbs in other places. Yogurts tend to be lower in carbs but they are still present. I will sound like a broken record, but carbs, in and of themselves, are not bad! We just need to make sure our shake stays protein-heavy.

As for the ice cream in the shake, I don't advise it. I also don't rule your pouches. But do the right thing, people!

The Protein Powder

What protein powder are you using? For the purposes of this check-up one kind of protein isn't as important as the stats. Yes, some proteins are more easily absorbed than others, but the ones we tend to use are about on equal playing fields. It's the stuff companies add to the protein powder to flavor it that can get us tripped up. Here are your questions there:

- How much fat is in my protein powder? Usually there isn't a lot.
- How many overall carbs? If you have a powder high in carbs, you're likely using a powder meant for bodybuilders. If you're unsure how to tell if your protein powder is meant for weight loss, talk with your registered dietician.
- How many of those carbs are sugar? Most decent protein powders have less than five grams of sugar.
- Where does the sugar come from? Look at the ingredients. If no table sugar is listed, and sugar can have many names, it is likely from the protein source which is likely to be lactose found in whey concentrate mixes.
- How much protein does it have relative to calories? Here, the 10:1 rule is a good one, in my humble opinion. If your protein powder doesn't have at least one gram of protein for every 10 calories, you need to re-think that protein powder. So a 120 calorie protein powder would need to have at least 12 grams of protein. Most powders have way more than that, some even having two grams of protein per 10 calories (the maximum amount possible per 10 calories).

Your Additives

This is where many of us get into trouble with protein shakes. Firstly, protein powder already has its own flavor additives. Secondly, if you're not careful, it's VERY easy to throw your shake stats off with just a little of something extra. Here, for what it's worth, are a few things I NEVER put in my protein shake (and what I use instead).

- A whole banana. Bananas are something of a sugar nightmare amongst fruits but they do have good nutrition which is why I still love them. If you must use banana, I'd suggest using half of one and freezing it. It ripens up and makes your shake really creamy. I use a tablespoon sugar-free banana cream pudding mix instead. You can also use sugar-free banana flavored syrup if you feel so inclined.
- Peanut butter, in ANY quantity. One tablespoon of peanut butter has 100 calories and 7.5 grams of fat. Need I say more? You have several substitution options. Some protein powders are peanut butter flavored. Then there is peanut flour, like PB2, and there is

sugar-free peanut butter flavored syrup. I suggest the former. But that's just me.

- Cream Cheese. Same deal as peanut butter. Too many calories, not enough protein given in return. If I want to make a cheesecake flavored shake I use sugar-free cheesecake flavored pudding mix. One tablespoon. BONUS TIP: to really make it cheesecake-y, give it a squirt of lemon juice or a packet of True Lemon. You'll be surprised what a difference it makes!

Other than that, just take into account how many extra calories you're adding to your shake. I'd also encourage you to think about your "return on investment." What I mean by that is you are taking a certain amount of extra calories but what are you getting for it? Sometimes your pay-out is not in protein. For instance, I use sugar-free pudding mixes to make my shakes thicker and creamier when I want them that way. I'm willing to pay the caloric price for that when the mood hits me.

The Big Picture

Ok, so you've looked at all the parts of your shake, now it's time to bring it all together.

Figure out the stats to your whole shake. Is it protein-heavy? Here's the scale I use for myself:

- Green light: WAY more protein (10 grams or more) than carbs or fat
- Yellow light: A bit more protein (six grams or more) than carbs or fat
- Red Light: The same amount of protein as carbs or fat or less

If you get into the yellow or red light district, go back and look at each of those components I described above. Think about what swaps you can make to bring your protein shake back to the land of the living.

Yes, this may seem like a lot to think about. I don't suggest doing this every day. But if you are in a stall, a protein shake check-up could very well help you out of it. It's important to be aware of what we put into our bodies!

Where to Buy

Here is information on where to buy various ingredients listed in this book.

BiPro Whey Protein

BiPro USA whey isolate protein powder is used in Nik's Baking Mix. To see the nutrition information for BiPro or to find it at a location near you, visit **biprousa.com**.

Sugar-free Syrups

While the two best known companies are Torani and Davinci, I should note there are other companies that make no-calorie flavored syrups, including:

- Starbucks: You can buy whole bottles of any of their sugar-free syrups at any of their locations so long as they have the bottles in stock. Visit **starbucks.com** for locations.
- SweetenFX: These syrups are good for people who choose not to consume sucralose, which is the sweetener used in both Torani and Davinci. Visit **naturesflavors.com/sweetenfx** to see flavors and learn where to buy.
- Various other brands that tend to pop up in stores like Home Goods, Tuesday Morning and Marshall's.

Torani syrups can be found in a wide variety of places online including their website, **torani.com**, but also on:

- Amazon: Good for Prime members, who get free shipping! Visit **amazon.com** to shop.
- Netrition: This site has myriad nutritional supplements and $4.95 flat rate shipping within the contiguous United States. Visit **netrition.com** to browse and shop.
- World Market: This store carries a variety of goods. You can browse their selection and find a location near you at **worldmarket.com**.

Davinci syrups can be found in a wide variety of places online including their website, **davincigourmet.com**, but also on:

- Amazon: Good for Prime members, who get free shipping!
- Netrition: This site has myriad nutritional supplements and $4.95 flat rate shipping within the contiguous United States. Visit **netrition.com** to browse and shop.
- Some Wal-Mart locations. Check the coffee aisle!

Powdered Peanuts

This ingredient can be found in a variety of places online. There are two main brands. Chike PB is made by Chike Nutrition (makers of Chike Protein) and can be found by visiting **ilikechike.com**. PB2 is manufactured by Bell Plantation and can be found on the Bell Plantation website, **bellplantation.com**, but also on Amazon, Netrition and in some grocery stores (see website for locations).

Italian Sweet Cream Coffee Creamer

This is made by CoffeeMate. Visit **coffee-mate.com** to check out their full selection and locate products near you.

High Protein Bread

The high protein bread tested in the French Toast recipe is made from P-28 bread. To find complete nutrition information for P-28 protein bread and find it in a store near you, visit **p28foods.com**.

The Bariatric Guide to Perfect Protein Drinks

This book is the most comprehensive collection of weight-loss surgery friendly protein shake recipes out there! Along with dozens of recipes it features tips on how to get your shake to *your* perfect texture as well as fun ideas on how to play with the form of your shake. It's available in hard copy and for Kindle from Amazon (visit **amazon.com**) and for Nook and iPad at Smashwords (visit **smashwords.com**).

While you're at it, both sites also carry *The Bariatric Foodie Holiday Survival Guide*, which is a collection of recipes, tips and tricks to survive the holidays. Be sure to pick up both so you have the full collection of Bariatric Foodie books.

Recipe Index

20117817R10092

Made in the USA
Middletown, DE
14 May 2015